Dene Nation – the colony within

MEL WATKINS is a member of the Department of Political Economy and University College at the University of Toronto, and was a consultant to the Indian Brotherhood of the NWT in Yellowknife.

This collection of papers by some twenty contributors has been selected in the main from presentations made to the Berger Inquiry, and reflects the efforts of the Dene people to block the construction of a pipeline through the Mackenzie Valley lands they claim as their own. The issue is broader than a pipeline or even a land claim, and the presentations go well beyond showing the adverse effects of a pipeline, serious though these may be, and beyond asserting an aboriginal claim to the land, valid though that may be. Rather, they reflect the Dene nation's fundamental perception that their struggle is for the most universal of human rights, the right to be a self-determining people, living with their land as they have always done. Should no pipeline ever materialize up the Mackenzie Valley, the Dene nation will continue to assert this right and continue to strive for decolonization in matters of economics, politics, education, law, and culture. The papers, some of them written by Dene and others by specialists in a variety of fields, reveal the profound issues of human rights from which pipeline protest ultimately derives. This book is essential reading for all concerned with Canada's future as a compassionate democracy.

'The publication is a lovely one: Informative, entertaining, and argumentative in a most responsible way. It isn't Watkins as author but Watkins as editor whom one must compliment. He's taken a score of essays or statements, including seven or eight by natives, and put them together into as good a single package as you need to understand why the issue of the pipeline from the far north is splitting our parties and symbolizing most of the world issues of environment, economic growth, natural resources and underdeveloped people.' Douglas Fisher, *Toronto Sun*

The cover photograph, by Tapwe Chretien, is of Dene playing a traditional handgame.

Dene Nation – the colony within

edited by Mel Watkins
for the University League for Social Reform

University of Toronto Press
TORONTO BUFFALO LONDON

© University of Toronto Press 1977
Toronto   Buffalo   London
Reprinted 1978, 1980, 1982
Printed in Canada

Library of Congress Cataloging in Publication Data

Main entry under title:
Dene Nation, the colony within.

A revision and abridgement of material presented at
the Mackenzie Valley Pipeline Inquiry (Berger Inquiry)
by the Dene themselves and by others on their behalf.
Bibliography: p.
CONTENTS: The Dene speak. – Dene declaration:
Blake, P., T'Seleie, F. & Lamothe, R. Statements to the
Mackenzie Valley Pipeline Inquiry. – Resources:
Nahanni, P. The mapping project. Snowshoe, C.
A trapper's life. Rushforth, S. Country food. Asch, M.
The Dene economy. Jellies, A.D. The loss of economic
rents. Helliwell, J.F. The distribution of economic
rents from a pipeline. Watkins, M. From undervelop-
ment to development. [etc.]
    1. Tinne Indians – Government relations – Addresses,
essays, lectures. 2. Indians of North America – Canada –
Government relations – Addresses, essays, lectures.
3. Pipe lines – Canada – Northwest Territories.
I. Watkins, Mel. II. University League for Social
Reform, Toronto.
E99.T56D46   323.1'19'707193   76-54701
ISBN 0-8020-2264-2
ISBN 0-8020-6315-2 pbk

Foreword

The University League for Social Reform has stimulated the publication of eight books on topics of public and intellectual concern since 1965. Typically, differing views have been expressed by the authors of each volume's various chapters, and the ULSR, as an organization, has taken no position on the issue under discussion.

In the case of *Dene Nation – The Colony Within*, the League feels it important to make a departure from its normal practice and explicitly support the essential positions that this book expresses on behalf of the Dene people:

1 The aboriginal right to self-determination claimed by the Dene is a universal human right; Canadians must therefore accommodate these demands within Confederation.

2 No pipeline project can be allowed before a land settlement is made with the native people. Such extracting of non-renewable resources before the achieving of a settlement would be to deny the Dene their right to self-determination.

3 The Dene are expressing their vision of an alternative society whose economy is based on renewable resources. It may be that this can coexist with the extraction of non-renewable resources, but it can only if the Dene are given back the power to control their own destiny.

Stephen Clarkson
PRESIDENT
University League for Social Reform

Contents

Preface

The Indian people of the Mackenzie District, who call themselves the Dene (pronounced 'Dennay'), today face the final onslaught of 'progress' in the form of applications to build a natural gas pipeline down the Mackenzie Valley through their homeland. To their great credit, the Dene are struggling mightily against these proposals. In the process, they are greatly strengthening their identity as a people and are once again asserting their rights as a nation. They are telling the rest of the world, and southern Canadians in particular, what colonialism has done to them and how they intend to decolonize themselves.

The government of Canada established the Mackenzie Valley Pipeline Inquiry under Justice Thomas R. Berger of the Supreme Court of British Columbia (the Berger Inquiry) to consider the separate proposals of the applicants, Canadian Arctic Gas Pipeline Ltd (Arctic Gas or CAGPL) and Foothills Pipe Lines Ltd, to build pipelines up the Mackenzie Valley. Arctic Gas proposes to bring both Alaskan gas and Canadian gas – to the extent that the latter exists – up the valley. Foothills proposes to bring only Canadian gas, but is willing to transport Alaskan gas via the Fairbanks corridor (or 'Alcan') route. The two routes up the valley vary somewhat, but for the Dene the differences are incidental. Either pipeline would pass through lands they have occupied and used since time immemorial. The land claim of the Dene is for these lands. It is with respect to these lands that the Dene have gone to the courts to endeavour to file a caveat to stop further 'development' that prejudices their claim.

Under these circumstances, the Dene have very properly made use of the Berger Inquiry to further their cause. The Dene themselves have spoken eloquently to Judge Berger, both at hearings in the Indian communities and at the formal sittings of the Inquiry in Yellowknife. They have enlisted the support of many non-Dene 'experts' in a variety of fields so as to translate their concerns into the language of the non-Dene.

In doing this, the Dene have gone beyond simply showing the adverse effects of a pipeline, serious though these would be. They have gone beyond

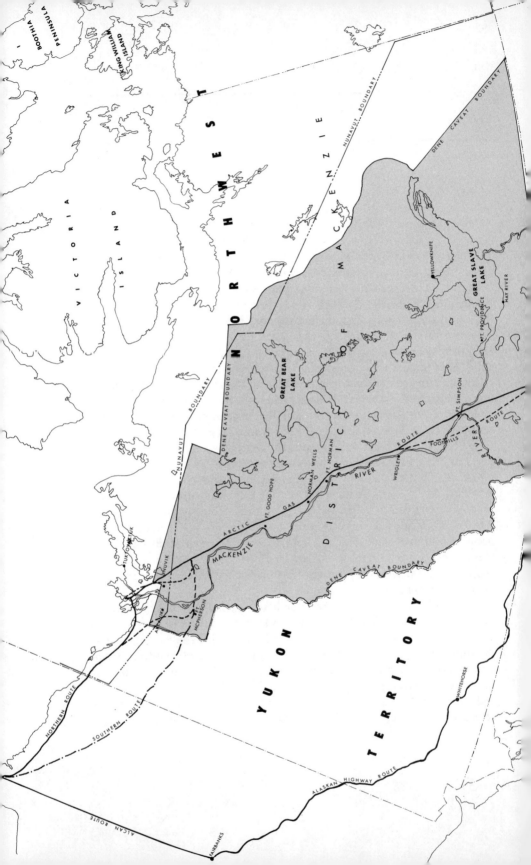

simply asserting their ownership of the land, real though that is, or should be. Rather, they have come to the fundamental perception that their struggle is for the most universal of human rights, the right to be a self-determining people. It is this right which the Dene insist the federal government must recognize as an integral part of aboriginal rights. The Dene have recognized the extent to which they have become a colonized people and they have begun to move down the long and difficult road to decolonize themselves. In their striving for liberation, they have understandably found sustenance in the increasingly successful struggles of colonized peoples elsewhere in the world.

This book reflects this perspective. It is based in large part on presentations made to the Berger Inquiry by the Dene themselves and by others on their behalf. It is, to reiterate, not just a book about a pipeline, or even about a land claim, but a book about the rights of the Dene nation. Should no pipeline ever materialize up the Mackenzie Valley, those rights will still be asserted by the Dene, and the rest of us will still have to come to terms with that fact.

While most of the material in this book was presented to the Inquiry, the book does not claim to reprint the transcripts of the Inquiry. Most presentations have been substantially shortened and in some cases revised. Readers who wish to know precisely what someone said to the Inquiry should consult the transcripts of the Inquiry. The concluding essay by Georges Erasmus, the President of the Indian Brotherhood of the Northwest Territories, is a very substantial revision, specifically for the book, of his presentation to the Inquiry in Fort Rae in August 1976. The paper by Professor Helliwell was prepared for presentation to the Berger Inquiry but ruled inadmissable; its obvious relevance warrants its inclusion here. The paper by Mr Sutton was written expressly for this book.

The book is drawn mostly from presentations made at the formal hearings of the Berger Inquiry and only in small part from the community hearings. Even with respect to the formal hearings, limitations of space have permitted the inclusion of only about one-third of the Brotherhood's witnesses. Readers who wish to read the evidence at the community hearings are referred to Martin O'Malley's excellent collection, *The Past and Future Land*.

On 25 October 1976, the Dene made public a proposal that a new Agreement be signed between the Dene and the Crown, an agreement that would supersede the Treaties and recognize the rights of the Dene nation. It has been included at the end of this collection, with excerpts from the Introduction to the Agreement as a preamble.

As editor of the book, I am, of course, responsible for its final form, but the book would not have been possible without the help of many people. I was myself privileged to work for the Indian Brotherhood in Yellowknife for two years and spent a good deal of my time assisting in the preparation of evidence for the Inquiry. But so too did many other people who were, or are, with the Indian Brotherhood. Many of them are included among the authors of this book; acknowledgements must also be made to the work of Richard Nerysoo, Glen Bell, Betty Menicoche, Evelyn LeMouel, and Pat Nelson.

I am grateful to the University League for Social Reform for sponsoring the book and in particular to its President, Stephen Clarkson, for his encouragement and advice. Editorial assistance was provided by Kelly Crichton; I have benefited greatly from her suggestions and judgment. Mrs Mary Rous of the Department of Political Economy, University of Toronto, was most helpful in making the University a pleasant place at which to edit this book. I join a long list of previous authors and editors of University of Toronto Press publications in acknowledging the wisdom of R.I.K. Davidson.

This book has been done with the encouragement and support of the Indian Brotherhood of the NWT. It is dedicated to the Dene.

M.W.
Toronto, Ontario
November 1976

The Dene Speak

Dene Declaration

Statement of Rights

We the Dene of the Northwest Territories insist on the right to be regarded by ourselves and the world as a nation.

Our struggle is for the recognition of the Dene Nation by the Government and peoples of Canada and the peoples and governments of the world.

As once Europe was the exclusive homeland of the European peoples, Africa the exclusive homeland of the African peoples, the New World, North and South America, was the exclusive homeland of Aboriginal peoples of the New World, the Amerindian and the Inuit.

The New World like other parts of the world has suffered the experience of colonialism and imperialism. Other peoples have occupied the land - often with force - and foreign governments have imposed themselves on our people. Ancient civilizations and ways of life have been destroyed.

Colonialism and imperialism are now dead or dying. Recent years have witnessed the birth of new nations or rebirth of old nations out of the ashes of colonialism.

As Europe is the place where you will find European countries with European governments for European peoples, now also you will find in Africa and Asia the existence of African and Asian countries with African and Asian governments for the African and Asian peoples.

The African and Asian peoples - the peoples of the Third World - have fought for and won the right to self-determination, the right to recognition as distinct peoples and the recognition of themselves as nations.

But in the New World the Native peoples have not fared so well. Even in countries in South America where the Native peoples are the vast majority of the population *there is not one country which has an Amerindian government for the Amerindian peoples.*

Nowhere in the New World have the Native peoples won the right to self-determination and the right to recognition by the world as a distinct people and as Nations.

While the Native people of Canada are a minority in their homeland, the Native people of the Northwest Territories, the Dene and the Inuit, are a majority of the population of the Northwest Territories.

The Dene find themselves as part of a country. That country is Canada. But the Government of Canada is not the government of the Dene. The Government of the Northwest Territories is not the government of the Dene. These governments were not the choice of the Dene, they were imposed upon the Dene.

What we the Dene are struggling for is the recognition of the Dene nation by the governments and peoples of the world.

And while there are realities we are forced to submit to, such as the existence of a country called Canada, we insist on the right to self-determination as a distinct people and the recognition of the Dene Nation.

We the Dene are part of the Fourth World. And as the peoples and Nations of the world have come to recognize the existence and rights of those peoples who make up the Third World the day must come and will come when the nations of the Fourth World will come to be recognized and respected. The challenge to the Dene and the world is to find the way for the recognition of the Dene Nation.

Our plea to the world is to help us in our struggle to find a place in the world community where we can exercise our right to self-determination as a distinct people and as a nation.

What we seek then is independence and self-determination within the country of Canada. This is what we mean when we call for a just land settlement for the Dene Nation.

This Declaration was passed at the 2nd Joint General Assembly of the Indian Brotherhood of the NWT and the Metis Association of the NWT on 19 July 1975 at Fort Simpson.

Phillip Blake
Fort McPherson
9 July 1975

My name is Phillip Blake and I am a treaty Indian from Fort McPherson. I have worked as a social worker in Fort McPherson for the past five and a half years.

First, I would like to say I am not an old man, but I have seen many changes in my life. Fifteen years ago, most of what you see as Fort McPherson did not exist. Take a look around the community now. And you will start to get an idea of what has happened to the Indian people here over the past few years.

Look at the housing where transient government staff live. And look at the housing where the Indian people live. Look at which houses are connected to the utilidor. Look at how the school and hostel, the RCMP and government staff houses, are right in the centre of town, dividing the Indian people into two sides.

Look at where the Bay store is, right on top of the highest point of land.

Do you think that this is the way the Indian people chose to have this community? Do you think the people here had any voice in planning this community?

Do you think they would plan it so that it divided them and gave them a poorer standard than the transient whites who come in, supposedly to help them? Take a look at the school here. Try to find anything that makes it a place where Indian values, traditions, and Indian culture is respected. It could be a school in the suburbs of Edmonton, Toronto, or Vancouver. Do you think Indian people would have chosen a building like this as a way to teach their children how to be proud of their Indian heritage?

Do you think Indian people chose to have their children taught that the only way to survive in the future is to become like the white man?

Look around you. Look at this building. Find out who the teachers are. Find out what they teach our children. Find out what regulations there are in this school, find out who decides these regulations, who hires the teachers, and who fires them.

This school is just a symbol of white domination and control. It is a part of a system set up to destroy Indian culture and to destroy our pride in our Indian heritage.

It is only part of that system. Look at some of the other parts. Do you think people chose to live in rental houses owned by the government, instead of in houses they built for themselves and owned by themselves? Do you think they chose to have a system of justice which often they cannot understand and which does not allow them to help their own people and deal with their own problems? A system which punishes the Indians for stealing from the Bay, but does not punish the Bay for stealing from the Indians? Do you think that they chose to become cheap labour for oil companies, construction companies, and government instead cf working for themselves and developing their own economy in their own way?

In short, Mr Berger, can you or anyone else really believe that we Indian people are now living the way we have chosen to live? Can you really believe that we have chosen to have high rates of alcoholism, murder, suicide, and social breakdown? Do you think we have chosen to become beggars in our own homeland?

Mr Berger, you are well aware that hundreds of years ago, in southern Canada and in the United States, many Indian civilizations were destroyed. In some cases, this was done simply by killing off the Indian people who occupied the land, the land that was valuable to white settlers. In other cases, it was done by restricting the Indians to small reserves where they could no longer hunt, fish, and make a living from their land. In all cases, it was pretty clear that whatever the white man wanted, the white man got. When he wanted greater land for farming, he cleared off the trees and he cleared off the Indians. When he wanted to dig the gold, or minerals from the land, he killed the Indians who tried to defend their own land.

In James Bay, when the white man decided that he wanted to again play God and change the course of mighty rivers, so he could make money and power from them, he corralled the Indian people into reserves and flooded the Indian land. The nations of Indians and Eskimos in the north have been slightly luckier.

For a while it seemed that we might escape the greed of the southern system. The north was seen as a frozen wasteland, not fit for the civilized ways of the white man. But that has been changing over the past few years.

Now the system of genocide practised on our Indian brothers in the south over the past few hundred years is being turned loose on us, and our Eskimo brothers. 'Don't be silly,' you may say. 'We are sorry about what we did in the past; we made some mistakes. But it's different now. Look, we give you an education, houses and health services.'

The system of genocide may have become a little more polished over the past few hundred years in order to suit the civilized tastes of the southern people who watch Lloyd Robertson on the National. But the effect is exactly the same. We are being destroyed. Your nation is destroying our nation. What we are saying today, here and now, is exactly what Louis Riel was saying roughly a hundred years ago.

We are a nation. We have our own land, our own ways, and our own civilization. We do not want to destroy you or your land. Please do not destroy us.

You and I both know what happened to Louis Riel. Yet now, a hundred years later, your Prime Minister is willing to say that Louis Riel was not all wrong. He is willing to say that a hundred years later. But is he willing to change the approach that destroyed Louis Riel? And his nation? And is now threatening to destroy us?

I am sure throughout your visits to native communities, Mr Berger, that you have been shown much of the hospitality that is our tradition as a people. We have always tried to treat our guests well; it never occurred to us that our guests would one day claim that they owned our whole house. Yet that is exactly what is happening.

White people came as visitors to our land. Suddenly they claim it as their land. They claim that we have no right to call it Indian land, land which we have occupied and used for thousands of years and which just recently the white man has come to visit. And suddenly he claims it to be his own.

Is this the great system of justice which your nation is so proud of? Now look at what happened to France during the Second World War. Germany moved in and occupied the land that France claimed as her own. At that time, Canada seemed willing to help a people whose land had been unjustly taken. Now, the same thing is happening to Indian nations of the north. Your nation has suddenly decided to move in and occupy land that is rightfully ours.

Where is your great tradition of justice today? Does your nation's greed for oil and gas suddenly override justice? What exactly is your superior civilization? How is it that it can so blindly ignore the injustice occurring continually over one-third of the land mass in Canada?

One-third of Canada is under the direct colonial rule. Yet you seem willing only to talk of igloos, polar bears and snow when you talk about the north. One has to read about South Africa or Rhodesia to get a clear picture of what is really happening in Northern Canada. While your newspapers and television talk about sports fishing up here, we as a people are being destroyed. And it barely gets reported in your TV or newspapers.

Look at us and what we stand for, before you accept without further thought that the Indian nation must die. In many parts of the world, people are starving. It is said that two-thirds of the people of the world go to bed hungry each night. We Indian people are sometimes accused of not being willing to share our resources. But what of this absurd scheme that Arctic Gas has dreamt up? What does it offer to those who are starving? Does it promise to use our resources and our land to help those who are poor? It suggests exactly the opposite.

It suggests that we give up our land and our resources to the richest nation in the world; not the poorest. We are threatened with genocide only so that the rich and the powerful can become more rich and more powerful.

Mr Berger, I suggest that in any man's view, that is immoral. If our Indian nation is being destroyed so that poor people of the world might get a chance to share this world's riches, then as Indian people, I am sure that we would seriously consider giving up our resources. But do you really expect us to give up our life and our lands so that those few people who are the richest and the most powerful in the world today can maintain and defend their own immoral position of privilege?

That is not our way.

I strongly believe that we do have something to offer your nation, something other than our minerals. I believe it is in the self-interest of your own nation to allow the Indian nation to survive and develop in our own way, on our own land. For thousands of years, we have lived with the land, we have taken care of the land, and the land has taken care of us. We did not believe that our society has to grow and to expand and conquer new areas in order that we could fulfil our destiny as Indian people.

We have lived with the land, not tried to conquer or control it or rob it of its riches. We have not tried to get more and more riches and power, we have not tried to conquer new frontiers or outdo our parents or make sure that every year we are richer than the year before.

We have been satisfied to see our wealth as ourselves and the land we live with. It is our greatest wish to be able to pass on this land to succeeding generations in the same condition that our fathers have given it to us. We did not try to improve the land and we did not try to destroy it.

That is not our way.

I believe that your nation might wish to see us, not as a relic from the past, but as a way of life, a system of values by which you may survive in the future. This we are willing to share.

If your nation chooses instead to continue to try and destroy our nation, then I hope you will understand why we are willing to fight so that our nation can survive. It is our world.

We do not wish to push our world onto you. But we are willing to defend it for ourselves, our children, and our grandchildren. If your nation becomes so violent that it would tear up our land, destroy our society and our future, and occupy our homeland, by trying to impose this pipeline against our will, then of course we will have no choice but to react with violence.

I hope we do not have to do that. For it is not the way we would choose. However, if we are forced to blow up the pipeline, I hope you will not only look on the violence of Indian action, but also on the violence of your own nation which would force us to take such a course.

We will never initiate violence. But if your nation threatens by its own violent action to destroy our nation, you will have given us no choice. Please do not force us into this position. For we would all lose too much.

Mr Berger, I believe it is because I am a social worker here that I have had to make some sense out of the frustration and desperation that people in this community and others along the valley are feeling. I have therefore tried to read as much as possible of other situations in Canada and in the world.

It is clear to me that the pipeline in Alaska has not been any part of progress, whatever progress may mean. Where progress should mean people getting greater control over their own lives and greater freedom, the pipeline in Alaska appears to have driven people into the ground, along with the pipeline.

Clearly, we do not want that here. Perhaps it is also because I am a social worker that I am aware what steps my people may take in reaction to the building of a pipeline here.

Mr Berger, it should be very clear by now what are the wishes of the people along the Mackenzie Valley regarding the pipeline here. I do not believe you or anyone else could misunderstand what the native people of this valley are saying.

Obviously, if we lived in any kind of a democratic system, there would be no further talk of the Arctic Gas pipeline. The will of the people has been made very clear. If this consensus, if the will of the people, is not respected, then I appeal to you and all people of southern Canada to respect and support us in our efforts to re-establish democracy and democratic decision-making in our homeland.

I guess the question for southern Canada is simply: which side are you on? Are you on the side of the people trying to find freedom and a democratic tradition? Or are you on the side of those who are trying to frustrate our attempts to find freedom and who are, instead, trying to destroy the last free Indian nation?

Mr Berger, I guess what I am really trying to say is: can you help us? And can we help you make sure that the will of the people is respected? After all, isn't that supposed to be what Canada once stood for?

Can we as an Indian nation help Canada to once again become a true democracy?

Statement to the Mackenzie Valley Pipeline Inquiry

René Lamothe
Fort Simpson
9 September 1975

I'm not born to the Dene people. My grandfather was a young man in 1885, and his older brother was one of five Metis killed defending Batoche. These men died at the hands of Canadian soldiers because they wanted to be citizens at par with eastern Canadians. This can be substantiated; it's in the Sessional Papers and in the Archives. These people died so that Canada would recognize their right to a piece of land from which to make a living. At Batoche the people, white, Metis, and treaty, sent petitions twice a year for fifteen years to the Canadian government to have title to their lands – just, you know, a quarter-section of land each. All they wanted was title to it, and for fifteen years their petitions were ignored. Now some few years later, however, in parts of Canada such as Alberta, Canada has recognized that right. In Alberta there are Metis colonies. The administration of Metis colonies is similar to the administration of reserves, only the administration of the colony is done from the provincial rather than the federal government level.

But this recognition came only after the Second World War when Canada had a strong peace-keeping force, a railroad to move troops if necessary, and economic control of the west through control of the agricultural sales. These realities were within the scope of Canada's plans from the time of Sir John A. Macdonald. He wrote, 'The Indians and Metis of the Northwest will be held down with a firm hand till the west is over-run and controlled by white settlers,' in a letter to a friend of his by the name of Rose; this letter is also contained in the Sessional Papers and the Archives.

Throughout this time and for generations before, the Metis had a love for the land that gave them the strength to die for it. That's where they wanted to live, and they were going to be run off and they said, 'No, we're not going to run again.'

Following generations, including my own, progressively lost this love to the extent that the Metis people as a people, when I was growing up, were very bland. I am married now into a family of the Dene people for close to five years. In those five years I have witnessed numerous examples of the love that the Dene have for this land.

As my capacity to love grew for my wife and children I began to acquire a capacity to love other things. I began to understand these examples I have witnessed of the love of the Dene for the land.

The love of the Dene for the land is in their tone of voice, a touch, the care for plants, the life of the people, and their knowledge that life as a people stems directly from the land. The land is seen as mother because she gives life, because she is the provider, the protector, the comforter. She is constant in a changing world, yet changing in regular cycles. She is a story-teller, a listener, a traveller, yet she is still, and when she suffers we all suffer with her; and very often in many parts of the world, whether they believe this or not, many people suffer because they have abused their land. She is a teacher, a teacher who punishes swiftly when we err, yet a benefactress who blesses abundantly when we live with integrity, respect her, and love the life she gives. We cannot stand on her with integrity and respect and claim to love the life she gives and allow her to be ravaged.

These are not threats. The people have not threatened violence. We are reacting to daily violence against us and our beliefs, and to threats of an ultimate act of violence from the south, an act so violent that, given the results of the petty violence which has been till now, it might be safe to say that a war of genocide by Canada against us would be less violent in terms of the next two to six generations.

Statement to the Mackenzie Valley Pipeline Inquiry

Frank T'Seleie
Fort Good Hope
5 August 1975

Mr Berger, as Chief of the Fort Good Hope Band I want to welcome you and your party to Fort Good Hope. This is the first time in the history of my people that an important person from your nation has come to listen and learn from us, and not just come to tell us what we should do, or trick us into saying 'yes' to something that in the end is not good for us. I believe you are an honest man. I believe you are a just man, Mr Berger, and that you do not intend to be a part of a plot to trick us or fool us or play games with us.

You are here on behalf of your government to ask us our opinions on the plans your people have for our land. Because you are honest and just, I do not believe you would be asking us these questions if your nation had already made a decision on these plans. It is not at all inevitable that there will be a pipeline built through the heart of our land. Whether or not your businessmen or your government believes that a pipeline must go through our great valley, let me tell you, Mr Berger, and let me tell your nation, that this is Dene land and we the Dene people intend to decide what happens on our land. Different people from outside have asked me whether or not I felt we could really stop the pipeline. My answer is: 'yes, we can stop the pipeline.'

Mr Berger, you have visited many of the Dene communities. The Dene people of Hay River told you that they do not want the pipeline because, with the present development of Hay River, they have already been shoved aside. The Dene people of Fort Franklin told you that they do not want the pipeline because they love their land and their life and do not want it destroyed. Chief Paul Andrew and his people in Fort Norman told you that no man, Dene or white, would jeopardize his own future and the future of his children. Yet you are asking him to do just that if you asked him to agree to a pipeline through this land. Phillip Blake, in Fort McPherson, told you that if your nation becomes so violent as to force a pipeline through our land, then we love our land and our future enough to blow up the pipeline. He told you that we, the last free Indian nation, are willing to fight so that we may survive as a free nation.

You have heard old people and young people, Mr Berger. You have heard people who were raised in the bush and people who were raised in government hostels. You have heard men and women, people who have worked for the whiteman, and people who have never sold their labour. People from the Mackenzie Delta to the Great Slave Lake. People have talked to you from their heart and soul, for they know, as I know, that if a pipeline goes through they will be destroyed.

All these people have told you one thing, Mr Berger. They have told you that they do not want a pipeline. My people are very strong and we are becoming even stronger. My people are finding new strength for the struggle that we are going through. That is why I can say to you, Mr Berger: yes, we can stop the pipeline. Our grandchildren will remember us, the Dene people here today, and the Dene people who have talked to you in other communities, as the people who stopped the pipeline from coming through their land.

Mr Berger, there will be no pipeline.

There will be no pipeline because we have our plans for our land. There will be no pipeline because we no longer intend to allow our land and our future to be taken away from us so that we are destroyed to make someone else rich.

There will be no pipeline because we, the Dene people, are awakening to see the truth of the system of genocide that has been imposed on us and we will not go back to sleep.

There will be no pipeline, Mr Berger, because we the Dene people will force your own nation to realize that you would lose too much if you ever allowed these plans to proceed. It is your concern about your future, as well as our concern about ours, that will stop the pipeline.

For our part, Mr Berger, we are making our own plans for the Dene nation. We are making plans not just for the next five or ten or twenty years, but plans that will guarantee the survival of our people for the next hundreds of years. We are making plans not just for ourselves, but for our children and our grandchildren and our grandchildren's children and for their children after them.

As you know, the Dene people recently held an assembly in Fort Simpson where we declared officially that we are a nation of people, within Canada.

For the Dene people, it was nothing very new or different to declare ourselves a nation. We have always seen ourselves in these terms. We have our own land, our own languages, our own political and economic system. We have our own culture and traditions and history, distinct from those of your nation.

I would like to read to you a copy of a letter dated 7 February 1928, addressed to the Director, Northwest Territories, Ottawa, from Father Binami:

Sir:

Due to the fact that Indians do their Fall fishing and trapping at points
north of Fort Good Hope and east of the Mackenzie River and as fish are not
obtainable at these places through the late Winter, they the Indians are forced
to move south and west to get moose and other game for food, we would suggest that two Preserves would be needed to do them good.

The two localities most frequented by them are bounded as follows:
1. From the mouth of the Hare Indian River east toward Smith Bay on Bear
Lake and North to the Junction of Anderson River and Lockhart Rivers then
west and south to New Chicago on Mackenzie River and South along the
Mackenzie River to the mouth of the Hare Indian River. New Chicago is at
the mouth of Tutsieta River.
2. From the mouth of the Gossage River west toward the Arctic Red River
and south along the Arctic Red River to a point west of the Sans Sault rapids
and North West of the Mackenzie River to the mouth of the Gossage River.

Locality No. 1 produces most food for the Indians and should be given
first consideration.

At the present time the Indians are in fear of too many outside trappers
getting into the districts outlined above and should these preserves be granted,
they, the Indians, would be more likely to endeavour to preserve the game in
their own way. They at present say they are afraid of leaving the Beaver colonies
to breed up as the white men would in all likelihood come in and hunt them.

Trusting this will receive your favourable consideration I remain,
Sincerely yours,
Father Binami, OMI,
For Indians and Petitioners

You can see from the letter, Mr Berger, that in 1928 we felt the same
about ourselves as we do now. We want to live our own way on our own land
and not be invaded by outsiders coming to take our resources. We saw ourselves then as we see ourselves now, as different from the whiteman. We do
not say we are better or worse than the whiteman. We are proud of who we
are, proud to be Dene and loyal to our nation, but we are not saying we do
not respect you and your ways. We are only asking now as we asked you
then, to let us live our own lives, in our own way, on our own land, without
forever being threatened by invasion and extinction. Mr Berger, we too want
to live. We want our nation to survive in peace, we want to be able to put our
energy and time into living our lives in the way our fathers and grandfathers
have taught us.

We do not want to have to fight and struggle forever, just to survive as a
people. Your nation has the power to destroy us all tomorrow if it chooses to.
It has chosen instead to torture us slowly, to take our children from us and
teach them foreign ways and tell us that you are teaching them to be civilized.
Sometimes now, we hardly know our own children. You have forced us into

communities and tried to make us forget how to live off the land, so you could go ahead and take the resources where we trap and hunt and fish. You encourage us to drink liquor until we are half crazy and fight among ourselves. What else other than liquor is the territorial government willing to subsidize to make sure that prices are the same throughout the Northwest Territories? Does it subsidize fresh food or clothing or even pop in the same way? No, only liquor. Try to buy anything else at Yellowknife prices throughout the North. The government knows very well that liquor helps keep my people asleep, helps keep them from realizing what is really happening to them and why. I know very well too, Mr Berger, because I used to drink. I am not the only one of my people who is waking up. There are many here in Good Hope who will be talking to you about their experiences. There are many, many more all over the Dene nation.

We are waking up and realizing that, apart from the glossy pamphlets and promises, apart from the smiles and slaps on the back, apart from the good-natured small talk, what your nation is really doing to us is destroying us. We know that now. And we know that you know it, for I believe that there are many white people in the North who did not realize before, that, whatever their personal feeling, the system that they were working for and supporting was really set up to destroy us. Many of these people honestly thought they could help us. It is clear now that the system is stronger than any individual. It is no accident that the territorial government is having great difficulty in recruiting people to work for it.

The individuals of your nation do not want to be part of your system of genocide.

There is a great force within your own nation to change the system under which you operate so that it becomes more human. These people are our allies. It is clear that there are many white men who believe that the Dene nation should survive.

Obviously Mr Blair, president of Foothills [who is present] and his friend Mr Horte, president of Gas Arctic, want to see us destroyed. Maybe, Mr Blair, that is because you do not know us or understand us. Or maybe money has become so important to you that you are losing your own humanity. Maybe you too are a victim, imprisoned by a way of life that you are afraid to question. I don't know. I only know you are a human being. There must be times when you too think of your children and their future. I doubt that you would knowingly destroy what is valuable to them. Why are you asking us to destroy our future? We are not trying to take your children and force them to speak a foreign language and to live out in the bush. Why are you trying to force us to be like you? Are you not rich enough now? Must you try to become so powerful to control our land and our children and our future? I cannot understand why you cannot be happy to live in a cabin beside some river and leave the world the way the Great Spirit made it. I cannot understand how a man can live for wealth and power, knowing that his ambitions and greed is destroying so much around him. I do not envy you, Mr Blair; I feel sorry for you.

Mr Blair, there is a life and death struggle going on between us, between you and me. Somehow in your carpeted boardrooms, in your panelled office, you are plotting to take away from me the very centre of my existence. You are stealing my soul. Deep in the glass and concrete of your world you are stealing my soul, my spirit. By scheming to torture my land you are torturing me. By plotting to invade my land you are invading me. If you ever dig a trench through my land, you are cutting through me. You are like the Pentagon, Mr Blair, planning the slaughter of innocent Vietnamese. Don't tell me you are not responsible for the destruction of my nation. You are directly responsible. You are the twentieth-century General Custer. You have come to destroy the Dene nation. You are coming with your troops to slaughter us and steal land that is rightfully ours.

You are coming to destroy a people that have a history of thirty thousand years. Why? For twenty years of gas? Are you really that insane? The original General Custer was exactly that insane. You still have a chance to learn, a chance to be remembered by history as something other than a fool bent on destroying everything he touched. You still have a chance, you have a choice. Are you a strong enough man to really exercise your freedom and make that choice? You can destroy my nation, Mr Blair, or you could be a great help to give us our freedom. Which choice do you make, Mr Blair? Which choice do you make for your children and mine?

It seems to me that the whole point in living is to become as human as possible; to learn to understand the world and to live in it; to be part of it; to learn to understand the animals, for they are our brothers and they have much to teach us. We are a part of this world.

We are like the river that flows and changes, yet is always the same. The river cannot flow too slow and it cannot flow too fast. It is a river and it will always be a river, for that is what it was meant to be. We are like the river, but we are not the river. We are human. That is what we were meant to be. We were not meant to be destroyed and we were not meant to take over other parts of the world. We were meant to be ourselves, to be what it is our nature to be.

Our Dene nation is like this great river. It has been flowing before any of us can remember. We take our strength and our wisdom and our ways from the flow and direction that has been established for us by ancestors we never knew, ancestors of a thousand years ago. Their wisdom flows through us to our children and our grandchildren to generations we will never know. We will live out our lives as we must and we will die in peace because we will know that our people and this river will flow on after us.

We know that our grandchildren will speak a language that is their heritage, that has been passed on from before time. We know they will share their wealth and not hoard it or keep it to themselves. We know they will look after their old people and respect them for their wisdom. We know they will look after this land and protect it and that five hundred years from now some-one with skin my colour and moccasins on his feet will climb up the Ramparts [near Good Hope] and rest and look over the river and feel that he too has a place in the universe; and he will thank the same spirits that I thank, that his ancestors have looked after his land well, and he will be proud to be a Dene.

It is for this unborn child, Mr Berger, that my nation will stop the pipeline. It is so that this unborn child can know the freedom of this land that I am willing to lay down my life.

Resources

The Mapping Project

Phoebe Nahanni

Our way of life is very ancient and enriching. Our economy is based on hunting, trapping, and fishing. Long before any non-Dene ever set foot on our land, our ancestors lived and learned from each other, from the land, and other beings on the land - the animals, birds, and insects. The mysteries of nature reveal themselves more and more through our experience on the land. Our way of life has been happening for a long, long time before any non-Dene ever set foot on this land, and it is still happening today.

From generation to generation our ancestors have passed on information by word of mouth, through legends and by relating personal experiences. The intricate values of our way of life are most appreciated by those who speak our languages. To the non-Dene such ways of recounting events may be subject to bias, error, misunderstanding, and misinterpretation. We Dene understand these shortcomings to be part of human nature.

Our people have withstood many seasons and many cycles. We consider our way of life to be the most practical for the climate and the environment we live in. Our songs, dances, games and legends are expressions and reflections of it. Here are the views of some trappers:

Willie MacDonald (65) at Fort McPherson, 13 January 1975:
But, wherever we go in the bush, we always see old signs, from long ago. We see old deadfall places and all this. We know that long before us this country been used lots and long time before that. People still using it. I mean the people that were brought up to the life of trapping and hunting. We belong to it, we belong to the land and we look at it like that land is our mother. That's where we're born and that's where we're going to go back. We're going to be part of this land when we die. There is no way we're going to leave it. That's why we think of this land. What else we got? Just land, land is our bank, it's our living, it's everything. Everything we got is this land. What we depend on next year coming is depending on this land. The land is the most precious thing we got.

Alexis Potfighter (75) at Detah, 15 September 1974:
The wild food gives us strength and faith, as far as it goes, for the whole Indian people. They gave us faith and strength to do anything ... Talking

about land, we're asking for the land to live on, to do things, like we're doing now, trapping. The land that we depend on must not stop. For we trap, hunt, and fish on the land that is ours. This is why our great ancestors handed to us to protect it from any damage in our land ...

Louis Moosenose (50) at Lac La Martre, 24 September 1974:
This land was given to us to make our living for food, clothing, and income ... The land was given to us to look after it and the land was supposed to be protected. The land, the water, and the animals are here for us to make living on it, and it's not to play with.

Amen Tailbone (60) at Rae Lakes, 30 September 1974:
The animals is our food, the land is our everything and the water is our drink, so the land is ours to keep as long as the sun is shining. The game wardens should not give hunting licences to their friends, because they do not kill animals for food, they kill animals for sports. The land, the water, and the animals are not here to play with. It was given to us to look after and protect it from enemies like white people. The white people are up to destroy everything they see, and the land is the only thing, we depend on it for everything, and it is not for sale.

In our culture, emphasis is placed on the importance of human beings, land and environment, and animals and birds. Without the land and environment and the animals and birds, we could not survive. This realization was not derived from nowhere; it was derived from years of experience and adaptation. And the land and animals cannot continue to live and survive without our understanding and respect.

This creation was produced neither from our intelligence nor from our hands. We are part of it. So are all animals, birds, fish, and insects. We all inhabit this environment (and ultimately this planet). Therefore, this realization is encouraged amongst us to ensure in the long run a continuation of resources.

When a human being occupies a space in the environment, his behaviour can be destructive or complementary to that space. (The former has been more evident since the white man moved on our land.) We understand that changes occur in human beings, environment, and in animals. These changes show in growth, seasons, and movement, and we are continually learning from this evolution through our experiences from our way of life. Our way of life has been tested over hundreds of years. It makes a lot of sense to us and we like to return to the land again and again, and we want our children to have the option to experience the same things.

Over the years we have observed the changes and the limitations placed on our freedom by the white peoples' government, the white peoples' laws, and white peoples' teachings. We did not write the laws that govern us and those that affect our way of life, such as the Migratory Birds Convention Act, Indian Act, Territorial Land Use Regulations, Game Ordinances, etc.; our silence in the past does not mean consent. We are participating in the white man's system not because we accept it, but because we have no choice. We regard our participation as being temporary until such time as our right to choose our own institutions is recognized.

There are debates all over Canada between the Indians and white people over many things. When we see that the present white institutions do not even suit many white people, we hope that will demonstrate the inability of these institutions to meet our needs. In many important respects our position in Canada today is a magnification of the experience of a vast number of Canadians.

While common experiences tie us to certain groups within Canadian society at large, many of our major problems stem directly from white peoples' ignorance of our differences. We believe a healthy society is not where we pretend such differences do not exist but one which recognizes and appreciates these differences and their contribution to the future development of society in general. A society as wealthy as Canada's which continues to perpetuate, even compound, the miseries of certain of its members is a sick society.

Land-use and occupancy research

For a year and a half the Indian Brotherhood of the Northwest Territories was involved in negotiating a proposal and budget with the Department of Indian and Northern Affairs to document data on traditional land use. At the time it was clear that no agency, government or private, was planning to undertake such a study. We knew that anthropologists and white researchers had previously attempted to integrate a study of our land-based activities into their theses. But our community leaders and community people expressed their dislike of the invasion of their privacy by outsiders who didn't speak their language. We know from our past experiences that government research by white researchers has never improved our lives. Usually white researchers spy on us, the things we do, how we do them, when we do them, and so on. After all these things are written in their jargon, they go away and neither they nor their reports are ever seen again. We have observed this and the Brotherhood resolved to try its best to see that, in future, research involves the Dene from beginning to end.

We got a commitment from DINA to fund the research for 1974-75 and 1975-76. Two years of research on a subject as old and continuous as our land-based renewable-resource economy could not possibly produce an exhaustive study. We therefore decided to work within the time constraints by obtaining a one-third sample, or approximately 30 per cent of the total number of trappers in each of five regions (Delta, North Mackenzie, South Mackenzie, North Slave, South Slave). Those trappers thirty years of age and over, we considered, would be best to provide us, from their substantial experience, with information on our economy. There are some exceptions to this, of course, judging from traplines covered by some hunters and trappers younger than thirty years of age.

The objectives of our land-use and occupancy research project were:

1. To form an information base upon which a just settlement of our grievances and land claims could be built, with an eye to securing our continuing benefit from the use of our land.

2. To provide a medium for re-establishing the bond between our young and their past, a bond essential to our future independence as Canadian citizens.

3. To provide us with material essential to us in deciding any action to be undertaken by us, in the event of a fair settlement, to improve our lot as we see fit.

4. To provide the people of Canada with a record of land use and occupancy in the Northwest Territories by people of Dene descent, from the distant past down to the present.

5. To provide the people of Canada with an understanding of the importance of our land to the integrity of our culture, our identity, and our present way of life, and to our future hopes.

6. To convey to the people of Canada the destruction inflicted on our civilization by the ethnocentric ignorance of the white man.

7. To give a truer appreciation of the costs of the present path of development the white man has chosen in the North, in terms of the Dene as a people with a right to survival *as a people*, and with a right to control and direct the changes the present and future force on them.

8. To give us an opportunity to present once again, without the confusion of middlemen, and in accordance with our own aims, the Dene experience and point of view as only we can present it.

Our main information source was to be the hunters and trappers themselves, and we held interviews in the following communities:

Delta Region: Aklavik, Inuvik, Fort McPherson, Arctic Red River
North Mackenzie: Fort Good Hope, Colville Lake, Fort Franklin, Fort Norman
South Mackenzie: Fort Wrigley, Fort Simpson-Jean Marie, Fort Liard, Nahanni Butte, Trout Lake, Fort Providence-Kakisa, Hay River
North Slave: Rae, Edzo, Lac La Martre (Marian Lake, Snare Lake), Rae Lakes, Yellowknife, Detah
South Slave: Resolution, Fort Smith, Snowdrift

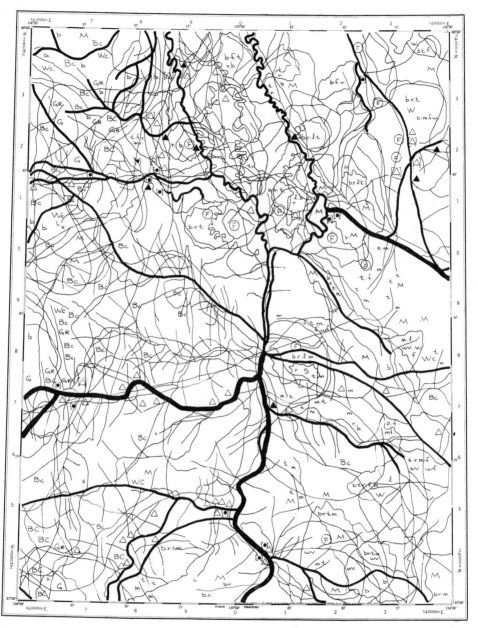

Sample map showing trails and traplines around Fort McPherson. It was compiled by the Mapping Project of the Indian Brotherhood of the NWT. One inch equals about twelve miles.

We wanted to gather information which could be represented on maps to show all the lands we have occupied at any time as far back as we can remember and also the situation at the present; how we used and use the land; and what the land means to us, as a people, at present. We asked such questions as When did you first begin to trap alone? Where did you trap? If you moved to other areas, why? What did you hunt and trap? Where did you fish? Where did you set up camps? What kind of camp? Do you go to this camp every year? How much does land mean to you? What are your views on land?

The greatest frustration we encountered in data collection, predictably, was the difficulty of locating the men we wished to interview; much of the time they were in the bush trapping, and were inaccessible to our researchers. This minor frustration was, of course, far outweighed by its positive aspect: the men's absence was additional empirical proof of the widespread continued use of the land that we had set out to document.

Another limitation we encountered was that it was simply impossible for every trapper interviewed to supply us with complete information on all his land-use activities throughout the years. There were various reasons for this: researchers could not spend as much time with each individual as would have been optimum; or informants grew too tired to continue an interview before they could impart the wealth of information they possessed to the interviewer. Therefore, we have been able to present only an outline of the present land-use patterns of approximately one-third of the men who are currently involved in hunting, fishing, and trapping. When looking at the sample map shown here, you must keep in mind that, even if you multiply in your imagination to three times the number of lines and routes indicated here, it still represents only partially the extent of use and occupancy of Dene lands by the Dene as it occurs today.

An important conclusion from our research is that there are approximately 1,075 men in the five regions actively engaged in hunting and trapping at the present time. We found that we could classify the traditional land uses as follows:

1 Subsistence hunting (all seasons from camps, e.g. moose hunting)
2 Seasonal hunting (e.g. caribou hunting)
3 Part-time hunting (all seasons based from a community)
4 Spring hunting and trapping (end of March through April to May for, e.g., beaver and muskrats)
5 Winter trapping (October-November to February-March for fur-bearing animals)
6 Fishing (all seasons)
7 Fishing (spring and/or summer at fish camps)

Dene people have considerable experience in surveying the environment we live in. Our ancestors travelled throughout the lands and, when the white men travelled on our land, it was with the advice and help of our ancestors. We have our own Dene place names for all our camps, for the lakes, the rivers, the mountains – indicating that we know the topography of our land intimately. Before Mackenzie came and claimed the river to be named after him, for example, we called it Deh-cho.

From the interviews we had with twenty-six young people, it is clear that there is a bond between young and old; that bond is essential to our future independence. The maps clearly show what the Dene have been saying all along before your legal institutions – that we have been here for hundreds and thousands of years; this is our land, and our life. This is the most graphic demonstration of the truth that we Dene own 450,000 square miles of land.

Our field work reinforces the statements made by the Dene at the community hearings of the Berger Inquiry that our attitude towards our land has far more substance than is fully appreciated by the oil and gas companies and government. That the proposed oil and gas pipeline routes and construction sites conflict with our land-based activities is obvious in the cartographic representation of those activities. These routes show no sign of regard for our trails, travel routes, and traplines, and our camps. The implications of such intrusions not only affect the trails, travel routes, and traplines; they also indiscriminately and without discretion affect the animals, fish lakes, and the environment and our way of life.

Producing these maps has been a lot of work. Over two years, about two dozen people have worked on this project and at any one time about a dozen people were working on it. The result is that data now exist on Dene land use that simply were not available before. Through the evidence of our land use and occupancy, we are showing that we have tolerated at great cost to our culture the kind of development thrust upon us, and from here on it is our right to control and direct the changes that affect our survival as a people.

A Trapper's Life

Charlie Snowshoe

I'm sorry to say that I had short notice of coming here [to Yellowknife to testify before the Berger Inquiry]. I was walking the street yesterday [in April 1976] thinking of getting ready to go out in the bush and I was met by Chief Johnny Charlie in Fort McPherson and he asked me if I would volunteer to come down here; I had no choice but to come because I'm interested in what's going on. I'm a little bit worried about being here right now. I live about 35 miles above Fort McPherson and it's getting pretty warm there. I'm worried about one creek because if the water starts in it before I get back I'm going to have to swim up it to get home.

I was in a residential school in Aklavik until I was fifteen years old. I got kicked out of school - I wasn't a dropout - for saying 'Go to hell' to the supervisor. I came back home and that same spring my dad got a registered trapping area. It wasn't really registered. It was just a sort of little place where we began to trap. My dad took me there and showed me a little bit how to trap rats - muskrats. And then I was told I had to go back to school again.

The next fall my dad took me up the Peel River to a place called Snake River. In Loucheux they call the Snake River 'gyuu dazhoonjik.' We went up one creek called 'Vakak deechyaa' creek. We went in this region through the fall. My dad showed me how to trap marten there. He just told me - he didn't take me out and show me - he told me to cross a lake in a straight line. I was a greenhorn in the bush at that time so when I crossed that lake like he told me, instead of making a straight line, I made a circle. That was my first experience with trapping.

We stayed there until Christmastime, and then from the Snake River, which is 150 miles above Fort McPherson, we went all the way up and back down that same winter. It wasn't very good trapping that winter so we went up to Rat River. We stayed there until Easter at a creek called Sheep Creek - 'divii daaghoonjik' in Loucheux. In March we came back down and moved to the Mackenzie Delta.

In the Delta there is all kinds of rivers and little creeks. There is a river called the Native River and a little creek which we call in Loucheux 'han gwa-jat' and in English it's called Rotten River. That is where we passed the spring and the next year we went up the Peel again. This time we went by dogteam. We crossed the Caribou Creek and we were following the old Dawson patrol trail to this area, which is called something like 'ah hjoutuk'; some hills there where it is good for marten.

After that we went back to McPherson at Christmastime. Then my dad moved me over to the mountain by Stoney Creek, halfway between Old Crow and McPherson. We travelled all winter, barely feeding dogs, and we never gave up. In those days, people weren't on welfare. We followed the caribou wherever they were going and we ran into some back at the mountain where we started. Then we went back to McPherson and back into the Delta again.

Every year around, this was what the old-timers had been doing – making all these markings on the maps. This is how the people at Fort McPherson and some from Aklavik trapped in this area. Until the fifties we did it like this. Then employment started coming in, so my dad and I worked in the summertime around McPherson and then in the fall we'd go back to hunting. It was routine then. In 1960 I got married and moved up to a creek. In English they call it Three Cabin Creek and in our language we call it Snit Lake. There is sort of a little delta there and lots of lakes.

We lived there year round, and one time between Christmas and New Years I had to go up to visit my lake which is about three days from the cabin. There was a couple of guys coming behind me and about six miles below I seen the smoke up there and there was no trail on the road. I was thinking 'What the heck is going on?' as I was going up and pretty soon I was getting puzzled. You know, I was confused. When I got to below that place there was a truck sitting with smoke from the exhaust going up in the air. I never heard of anybody working in that area. So I went up and asked them, 'What are you guys doing?' When he said 'seismic lines,' I didn't know what he meant. And that's the way it has been started. Nobody knew what was going on.

After the seismic lines started, I still stayed in the bush with my brother-in-law. But in 1970 I started thinking about wages. I was in school until I was fifteen and I had grade 7 so a lot of times while I was trapping, I was saying, 'gee whiz, I shouldn't be doing this. I should be in school. Maybe I should try to get a job and sit in an office and drink coffee like the other people.' So that's what I did. I went into town and applied for training. I thought I was doing myself a favour, but I wasn't.

Anyway, I put an application in for training as a heavy duty driver. But I couldn't get it because I didn't have enough grades, so they asked me if I wanted to go into an upgrading school. When I left the school they offered me a job and I got the office job. But when I was trying that, I was getting lonesome for my land. And I was lonesome especially when there was nice sunshine outside and all the rats were swimming around and the ducks flying around.

That's when they started coming in with these low rental housing and welfare. The people, the native people of the north, were independent until you brought in that low rental housing, and that's where we first got sucked into that business. They subsidized the oil, the gas, taking our own houses away from us, moving us from where we used to be, where we could cut wood for ourselves in town. We were working every day then, not like today. That's the start of spoiling people. I was one of them. Today I'm sorry. I was sorry long ago, but right now if I move out of that house, I don't know where else I have to go to. I have six kids at home. But we are thinking of getting our own house and starting to burn wood – we are not worried about oil. I don't know about the other communities, but in Fort McPherson we are trying to do away with a lot of these things right now and we are going back to the bush slowly.

When I first started working in town there was booze, and liquor came free to all of us as long as we had money and I became an alcoholic. I was lucky enough to hang onto a job. But now I haven't drunk for over a year and I still try my best. Last spring I was working on the Dempster Highway and I didn't like what I saw concerning us natives. From there I went in and worked in the co-op store and then I said, 'No way, I'm not going to work, I'm going to go back in the bush and fish.' And that's what I did last summer.

In January I got a job working with alcoholics. We got a little centre in McPherson and I'm glad to help, seeing that we're trying to show that we are trying to help ourselves. I'm working at that now, but I asked for a month off so I can go out hunting rats. I'm supposed to be gone already, but I'm here. Right now, I'm worried like I said; I've got to get back home. Maybe I'm going to have to charter a plane and charge it up to Gas Arctic or Foothills.

We are screaming about our land and we don't want the pipeline to come through. Now Judd Buchanan ok'd for them to drill up here [in the Beaufort Sea]. This is the main source, the main place where the fish are always coming. Our people depend on that fish, and if we have a blowout, goodbye fish. That's why we don't want it.

The only thing I can say is the change in life sort of crept upon us and we are realizing now what we got into. At the time, everything was changing, and I used to say we were sleeping the time government stepped over us. But we weren't sleeping. We were out living in the bush and we didn't know what was going on in the community; when we'd get back into the community, we heard a little of this and that, but we didn't stay in the community. One month at a time, we used to stay there around Christmas and New Year. About a week after New Year, everybody would leave.

All these new things came upon us - like education and working. We realize now that our way of life was good when we used to stay in the bush. We are trying, we are going back slowly.

Country Food

Scott Rushforth

Developers, such as the pipeline applicants, frequently allege that the Dene no longer rely substantially on country food derived from traditional use of the land. I have been studying the recent land use of the Great Bear Lake Indians, or Dene, of Fort Franklin, but the findings very probably apply to the Dene in general.

The Bear Lake people, or 'Sahtúgot'ine,' derive their name from the lake at which they live. Their ancestors occupied a territory extending around the entire shore of the Great Bear Lake. Their cultural affiliations are with Slave, Hare, and Mountain Indians along the Mackenzie River and with Dogrib Indians south of Great Bear Lake. Their language belongs to the Athapaskan family and is a dialect of the Slavey language which is spoken throughout much of the Northwest Territories.

Today, the Bear Lake people have their houses at the hamlet of Fort Franklin which is located near the mouth of the Great Bear River approximately ninety miles from the Mackenzie River settlement of Fort Norman. Like their ancestors, they must organize their way of life so as to cope with conditions imposed upon them by their subarctic environment. In addition, they must now cope with conditions increasingly imposed upon them by forces outside of their land, that is, they are faced with acts, objects, and events which originate in socio-cultural systems far from the Great Bear Lake but which, nevertheless, have a tremendous impact upon them and their traditional way of life.

Recent land use by the Great Bear Lake people

TRAPPING

Mid-October to Christmas and January to February are times for trapping around the Great Bear Lake. The most intensive period of trapping is during November and December; fewer men go to the bush after the New Year. At the Bear Lake the most important fur-bearing animal is the marten, with fox (all species), lynx, and other animals also of importance.

When a man from Fort Franklin goes into the bush to trap today he normally leaves his family behind in Fort Franklin and travels with a friend or relative. He must outfit himself with traps, clothing, snowshoes, guns (a .22 and 30-30), a tent and stove, a bedroll, a snowmobile or dogs, a toboggan, a fish net, sundry tools and utensils, and food – especially tea, flour, sugar, and lard. His total investment will normally be in excess of $1,800. Bear Lake men do not, of course, make this total investment every trapping season as many of their goods are usable for a number of years. However, the cost of capital goods required by them for their subsistence activities is very high. The fact that they continue to invest in such capital goods is in itself an index of the importance to them of a bush-oriented life. Also, many Bear Lake men view wage labour not as a permanent alternative to traditional land-use activities but solely as a means of obtaining the tools they require in the bush.

In addition to men who trap on a full-time basis, many men who have jobs, or some other reason for remaining in Fort Franklin, trap on a part-time basis. These latter men usually have a snowmobile for rapid transportation to their weekend camps and traplines which extend as far as thirty miles from Fort Franklin. By trapping every weekend, they are able to supplement their wage income with some fur sales; catch a few rabbits with snares; shoot a few ptarmigan or grouse; and bag an occasional woodland caribou. Perhaps more important than this, through such activity these men remain attached to a bush-oriented life style. Such part-time trapping makes the Fort Franklin region quite important in the total pattern of trapping. Other areas which have been trapped extensively during the last five years include the Edacho-Mackintosh Bay-Tuitatui region, the Johnny Hoe region, and the Whitefish River region.

If a man is using dogs while trapping he will normally leave Fort Franklin somewhat earlier in the season than if he has a snowmobile and will set his camp near a fish lake such as Tuitatui or near the mouth of a river such as Johnny Hoe River. In this way, he can set nets, take advantage of the late October runs of whitefish, and be assured of food for both himself and his dogs. The length of time he keeps his nets in the water depends upon the productivity of his nets and upon his own requirements in the bush. His own needs depend upon how many dogs he has and upon the length of his stay on the trapline. He will keep his nets in the water until he has enough fish for himself and his dogs and, perhaps, can send some back to Fort Franklin.

In addition to fishing while on their traplines, men are able to spend time hunting for moose and woodland caribou. Of course, whenever men check their traps they carry a gun with them. In this way, during the 1974-75 trapping season, at least ten woodland caribou and four moose (in addition to those caribou killed by part-time trappers) were taken by the Bear Lake people.

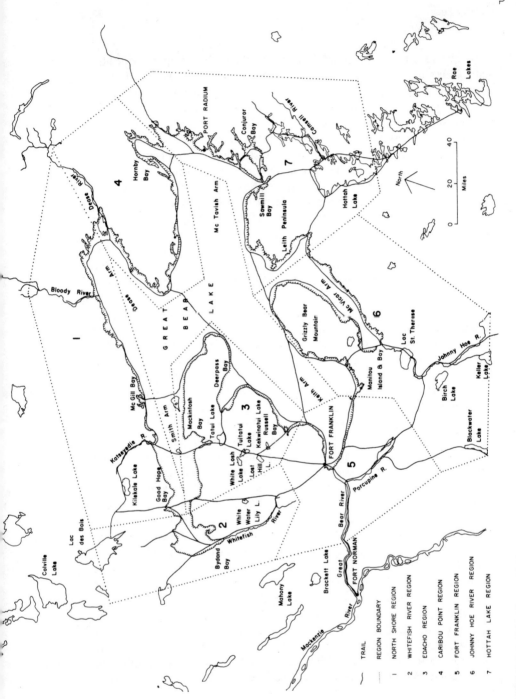

PORT RADIUM

Conjuror Bay

Camsell River

Roe Lakes

Hornby Bay

4

Mc Tavish Arm

Sawmill Bay

7

Dease River

Leith Peninsula

Hottah Lake

Bloody River

North

Dease Arm

G R E A T   B E A R   L A K E

Mc Vicar Arm

Grizzly Bear Mountain

40

20

0

Miles

McGill Bay

Smith Arm

Mackintosh Bay

Deepass Bay

6

Lac St. Therese

Johnny Hoe R.

Katseyedie R.

Totui Lake

3

Tuitatui Lake

Kekwinohtui Lake

Russell Bay

Keith Arm

Manitou Island & Bay

Keller Lake

Kilekale Lake

Good Hope Bay

White Losh Lake

Lost Hill L.

FORT FRANKLIN

Birch Lake

Loc des Bois

2

White Woter L.

Lily L.

River

5

Porcupine R.

Blackwater Lake

Colville Lake

Bydond Bay

Whitefish River

Bear River

Mahony Lake

Brackett Lake

Great

FORT NORMAN

Mackenzie River

TRAIL

REGION BOUNDARY

1   NORTH SHORE REGION

2   WHITEFISH RIVER REGION

3   EDACHO REGION

4   CARIBOU POINT REGION

5   FORT FRANKLIN REGION

6   JOHNNY HOE RIVER REGION

7   HOTTAH LAKE REGION

1

CARIBOU HUNTING (BARREN-GROUND AND WOODLAND)

Traditionally, Bear Lake people relied upon caribou, especially the barren-ground caribou, for a large portion of their food as well as for many of their technological needs. Today, they utilize Western clothing, shelters, and tools. However, caribou is still essential as a source of food and as a source of hides for mittens, footwear, babiche, and handicrafts.

There are essentially two kinds of caribou hunting at Bear Lake today: community-organized hunts for barren-ground caribou during the spring and summer; and individually organized hunts for both species of caribou at all times of the year. Community-organized barren-ground caribou hunts (supported by the Game Management officials of the government of the Northwest Territories), have occurred in February and March and in August during the seventies and have normally lasted from three weeks to one month. Spring caribou hunts have been by snowmobile and dog team to the Hottah Lake and Caribou Point regions at the east end of the lake, with exceptions to this in 1971 and 1972 when men from Fort Franklin joined men from Fort Norman on hunts to the Colville Lake and Kilekale Lake regions, respectively. Summer caribou hunts have been by canoe to the North Shore of Great Bear Lake.

During the spring and summer hunts, men shoot caribou for both the community freezer and for themselves. Community meat is transported by bombardier, by the community's large fishing boat, and by chartered aircraft. Individual hunters' meat is transported by the hunter in his own toboggan or canoe.

In February and March 1975, two trips to the east end of the lake for caribou were made. The first of these was to Caribou Point for ten days and involved five men. The second was to the Port Radium region for three weeks and involved twenty-seven men. On these hunts, Bear Lake people took at least 165 barren-ground caribou and three moose. About ninety of the caribou were placed in the community freezer for distribution among all of the Bear Lake people, with the remaining seventy-five or so going to individual hunters' families.

During August 1974, approximately twenty-five men (many of them with their wives and children) went to McGill Bay on the North Shore of the lake to participate in the summer hunt. Not only was this hunt viewed as a chance to obtain food, but also as an opportunity for many of the men to take their families out onto the land. While men went hunting each day, women remained in camp to scrape and tan hides, to make dry meat, and to tell stories to their children. When all of the men went out together for two day's hunting fifty miles east of McGill Bay, women and children took over the entire operation of the camp, including getting firewood and hunting ptarmigan. In all, approximately 120 caribou were taken, in spite of the fact that hunting was cut short by a week or ten days.

Individually organized caribou hunting for both barren-ground and woodland caribou takes place very frequently. Two, three, four, or more men will hunt together on their own initiative at places all around the Bear Lake. In summer, men take advantage of the fact that woodland caribou often come down to the shore of the Bear Lake to escape from flies and mosquitoes in the bush. While travelling along the shore in canoes, towards Grizzly Bear Mountain, for example, men can hunt these caribou very conveniently. By taking their fishing poles along with them on such trips men can bring back to their families ten or twenty lake trout in addition to or in place of caribou.

Individually organized caribou hunting also takes place during the fall and winter while men are trapping. When checking their traps, men often run across fresh caribou tracks and, if weather and conditions are right, immediately set out after the caribou. If they are able to shoot an animal, trappers eat some of the meat themselves, but send much of it back to Fort Franklin to feed their families.

SPRING BEAVER HUNTING

During May men from Fort Franklin go to inland rivers and lakes to hunt with .22s for beaver and muskrat. From the spring beaver hunt they get fur to sell and plenty of meat to eat. Camp is not necessarily set near a fish lake, since there are beaver, muskrats, and water fowl for food. Meat which is not consumed in the bush is dried and brought back to Fort Franklin in pack sacks.

Like trapping, spring beaver hunting is now an activity almost exclusively for men. School is still in session so women normally stay in Fort Franklin with their children. Men travel together as partners with other men or with their older sons. A man and his partner hunt together or separately but divide their kill of beaver between them so that nobody is 'short.'

Areas which have been very important for spring beaver hunting during the five years under consideration include the Tuitatui region, the Whitefish River region, the Johnny Hoe region, and the Porcupine River region. Men select their locations for beaver hunting on the basis of a knowledge of the land, signs of beaver seen during the previous trapping season, and a knowledge of where and when other hunters have been during the recent past.

FISHING

Fishing is, and always has been, a major source of food for the Bear Lake people. For eight or nine months of the year, depending upon ice conditions, they are able to set nets and catch very large numbers of lake trout, whitefish, herring, and grayling. Such fish are used for human consumption, but also provide the bulk of food for dogs. The amount of fishing a man does is tied to both his own needs and the number of dogs he owns.

Fishing while on trapping trips has already been noted; it occurs at Johnny Hoe River, Mackintosh Bay, Deerpass Bay, Good Hope Bay, and fish lakes such as White Water Lily Lake, Tuitatui, and Lost Hill Lake. Late October, November, and December are the months of the year for this fishing, which is primarily for whitefish.

Fishing in the Great Bear Lake near Fort Franklin occurs throughout the entire year except during freeze-up and break-up. Men fish at Fort Franklin primarily for lake trout and herring. During the months from December to May men fish for trout and herring under the ice using gill nets for both kinds of fish and set hooks for trout. Trout productivity is down during these months, but large numbers of herring are caught by men setting nets near the mouth of the Great Bear River which remains free of ice throughout the winter.

During May those men who have nets under the ice watch the ice and weather closely so they can remove their nets before the ice gets too thin and breaks up. Men with nets by the Bear River must take them out relatively early since flowing water there melts the ice quickly. By the first or middle of June all nets and hooks are out of the water and ice is rapidly leaving the lake. By early July the ice is normally gone and men reset their nets in the open water.

From July to September trout production is up and men catch hundreds of these large fish in nets and on hook lines. Herring nets are set close to the shore but fewer of these fish are caught than in the winter. During the summer men also fish nowadays with rod and reel for trout and grayling. In July especially a trip to the Bear River by canoe can result in fifty or a hundred grayling. Trolling for lake trout within ten or fifteen miles of Fort Franklin is not only enjoyable, but normally results in ten or twenty fish per boat.

Bear Lake people also make seasonal trips to places such as Deerpass Bay, Russell Bay, Caribou Point, and Johnny Hoe River for the purpose of setting nets and establishing fish camps. All of these places were very important to them in the past (as were places such as Bydand Bay, Mackintosh Bay, Dease Bay, and Sawmill Bay) as fisheries and as locales of relatively continuous occupation and use. During trips to these places men can catch hundreds of fish in a very short time.

MOOSE HUNTING

Moose hunting takes place most often while men are trapping or caribou hunting. However, men also go to the bush specifically to hunt moose during the fall and winter. In September 1974, for example, six men made a five-day trip to Grizzly Bear Mountain to hunt moose and set nets. They returned with two moose, a load of fish, and about a hundred ducks. In February 1975, at least five trips for moose were made around the Bear River and towards Whitefish River. On these hunts, seven moose were taken. In all, seventeen moose were taken by Bear Lake people during the year 1974-75.

Areas around the Bear Lake which are used for moose hunting include Johnny Hoe River, Grizzly Bear Mountain, Great Bear River, Porcupine River, and Whitefish River.

BIRD HUNTING

Great Bear Lake people, although not relying to any great extent upon bird hunting, do take a certain number of duck, ptarmigan, and grouse for food. Such birds provide a welcome break from their normal diet of fish, caribou, and store-bought food. The number of birds taken during 1974-75 is estimated as 1,500 to 2,000 ducks, 750 to 1,100 ptarmigan, and 250 to 350 grouse.

Participation in traditional land-use activities

During the years 1970-71 to 1974-75, there were 52 adult male household heads (out of a total of 54) in Fort Franklin who could possibly participate in the four main kinds of primary subsistence activity – trapping, barren-ground caribou hunting, spring beaver hunting, and fishing. There was thus a total of (52 x 4) 208 possible units of land-use activity for adult male household heads during any given year. By totalling the number of different kinds of activities in which these men, in fact, participated during a given year and computing that figure as a percentage of the total possible units of activity, a figure is obtained which can be used as an index of general or overall traditional land use at Bear Lake. By computing such percentages for each of the five years under consideration, general trends in subsistence activities at Bear Lake can be determined, as shown in Table 1.

A number of facts are revealed therein which warrant comment. First, the number of men who trap each year has remained relatively constant. This is an important finding in light of the further fact (based on fur export returns) that the number of fur-bearing animals harvested from 1972-73 to 1974-75 declined. The latter can be attributed to low fur prices which caused Bear Lake men to put less effort into trapping, for example, tending not to return to the bush for January and February after spending Christmas in Fort Franklin. That the same number of men nevertheless continue to trap is indicative of the values attached to participation in bush-oriented activities.

TABLE 1
Summary of participation by adult male household heads
in four primary kinds of land-use activity for the years 1970-71 to 1974-75.

	1970-71	1971-72	1972-73	1973-74	1974-75	Five-year average
Men trapping	31	29	35	35	28	
Men hunting barren-ground caribou	10	12	24	19	36	
Men on spring beaver hunt	26	24	36	24	11	
Men fishing	27	25	28	27	28	
Total participation	94	90	123	105	103	103
Total participation as percentage of maximum participation ($n = 208$)	45	43	59	50	50	50

Second, there has been a significant increase in the number of men engaged in caribou hunting. The undiminished value attached by Bear Lake men to traditional land-use activities continues to provide them with the motivation to participate in these hunts. The availability of and acceptance by Bear Lake men of new kinds of technology (e.g., chartered aircraft) and new kinds of group organization (e.g., hunting groups organized by the Band Council and Hamlet Trappers Association) has increasingly enabled them to exploit caribou herds hundreds of miles from Fort Franklin. As well, support from Game Management has provided the capital required by the Bear Lake men to pay for, among other things, transportation costs.

Third, there has been a decline in the number of men participating in spring beaver hunting. This relates directly to the declining price of beaver pelts during the 1974 and 1975 seasons. However, many men who did not go beaver hunting during these years replaced this activity with another traditional land-use activity – establishing spring fish camps. For example, during spring 1974 six men established fish camps rather than going beaver hunting.

Fourth, there has been no significant change in the number of men fishing during the years 1970-71 to 1974-75. Fishing continues to be a dominant activity of the Bear Lake men and continues to provide tremendous amounts of food.

The fifth and final fact is that there has been no general or over-all decrease in the numbers of Bear Lake men participating in traditional land-use activities. Based upon the information I collected, Bear Lake people are simply not abandoning their traditional means of making a living.

And neither are they abandoning their traditional territory. Although the Bear Lake people no longer live in small dispersed groups throughout their

TABLE 2
Approximate replacement value of food obtained through traditional subsistence activities and trapping income of the Bear Lake people during the year June 1974 to May 1975.

Species	Replacement dollar value/pound	Approximate total edible weight (in pounds) of species harvested	Approximate dollar value
Barren ground			
caribou	2.40[a]	22,800	54,720
Woodland			
caribou	2.40	2,000	4,800
Moose	2.40	9,900	23,760
Fish:			
Lake trout	1.50 / .35[b]	39,360– 54,960	47.724– 66,639
Whitefish	1.50 / .35	30,400– 36,400	28,120– 33,670
Herring	1.50 / .35	30,200– 48,320	19,252– 30,804
Grayling	1.50 / .35	6,000– 9,000	3,825– 5,737
Birds:			
Ducks	1.30[c]	2,250– 3,000	2,925– 3,900
Grouse	1.30	250– 350	325– 455
Ptarmigan	1.30	375– 550	487– 715
Total (lb.) of species harvested		143.535–187,280	
Total replacement value of country food			185,938–225,200
Fur trapping income			21,707[d]
Total income from traditional activities			207,641–246,907
Total food requirements[e]		445.092–539,152	

a The $2.40 replacement value for caribou is based upon the average cost of beef in Fort Franklin.

b The $1.50 figure is the replacement value of fish which is consumed by humans. The $.35 figure is the replacement value for fish consumed by dogs. It is estimated that 75 per cent of the lake trout caught are consumed by humans; 50 per cent of the whitefish caught are consumed by humans; and 25 per cent of the herring and grayling caught are consumed by humans.

c The $1.30 replacement value for birds is based upon the average cost of chicken in Fort Franklin.

d This estimate does not include dollar values for certain things, for example, handicraft production, which in a more complete report would be included in income derived from traditional land-use or land-use related activities.

e Computed following John Stager, 'Old Crow, YT, and the Proposed Arctic Gas Pipeline' (1974). Approximate resident population of Bear Lake people is: adult men, 79; adult women and adolescents, 139; children, 135. Food requirements for the year were computed according to the following table listing pounds of food per day required by people:

	Minimum	Maximum
adult men	4	5
adult women & adolescents	3.2	4
children	2	2.5

Dog food requirements were also computed following Stager and amount to 425 pounds of food per dog per year. There are approximately 162 dogs in Fort Franklin.

land at places such as Johnny Hoe River, Caribou Point, Dease Bay, Bydand Bay, and Mackintosh Bay, they continue to use all of these and other locations for their hunting, trapping, and fishing. At many of these locations cabins have been built and camps are maintained for seasonal use throughout the year. The people continue to use the entire area of land they inhabited twenty-five years ago. Every year they have trapped throughout their land, hunted caribou at the North Shore and around Hottah Lake, and fished at Fort Franklin, Deerpass Bay, Johnny Hoe River, and Mackintosh Bay.

Income from the land

Some idea of the dollar value of land-use activities can be derived through, first, an estimate of the dollar value of products derived from traditional activities and, second, an estimate of the amount of food derived from the land as a percentage of the total amount of food required. The dollar value of traditional economic activities for 1974-75 includes income from furs as well as the value of food, but we are concerned here mainly with food.

In assigning a dollar value to food from the land, the 'replacement value,' that is, the cost in dollars of replacing that food with food obtained from other, 'non-traditional' sources (for example, the Hudson's Bay Company), of that food is used. A simple 'replacement value' is used in spite of the fact that 'country food' has several characteristics which make it even more valuable than the food with which it is replaced. Caribou meat, for example, has the following characteristics: (1) it is invariably preferred over beef by the Bear Lake people both for its taste and because it is 'native-grub' and not 'white-grub'; (2) caribou has a higher protein content per unit than beef; and (3) caribou (and other meat from the land) is more important to the diet of the Bear Lake people since it is often replaced, not by protein-rich food such as beef, but by food high in carbohydrates.

Using the 'replacement value' of food obtained from the land, the figures reported in Table 2 result. It is estimated that, including cash income from fur sales, the equivalent of between $200,000 and $250,000 in income was derived by the Bear Lake people from their land during the year 1974-75. This figure represents a 'per household income' of between $3,200 and $3,900 (based on the total number of households at Fort Franklin – 64) and a 'per capita income' of between $580 and $700 (based upon a total native population of 353).

An estimate of the contribution of country food to the total food requirements of the Bear Lake people (and their dogs) can be obtained by estimating the minimum and maximum food requirements for these people and comparing those figures to minimum and maximum estimates of subsistence food-production. (Dogs are included in this figure because dog teams are an essential part of the capital investment of the Bear Lake people. Even men who have purchased snowmobiles recognize that these machines are less reliable than dogs and many of them own dog teams and use them for more extended trips to the bush. Snowmobiles break down – and there are no gas stations at Tuitatui.) On this basis it is estimated that from 27 to 42 per cent of their food requirements were met by the Bear Lake people in 1974-75 through traditional subsistence activities.

The historical and cultural context

From the early 1800s until the 1950s when the Bear Lake people settled at Fort Franklin, they hunted, fished and trapped at all of the places cited previously. People from Bear Lake also travelled to Rae, Coppermine, the Mackenzie Mountains and Fort Good Hope while making their living. For the most part, however, they stayed within their own land and traded at Fort Norman or one of the various posts established intermittently at the Great Bear Lake.

In 1920 oil was discovered at Norman Wells, a little over 100 miles from the Bear Lake. In 1921 and 1922 the Bear Lake people signed Treaty 11 at Fort Norman, where they usually had gone to trade during summer, thus becoming drawn into a trading economy – tea, flour, sugar, lard, guns, axes, ice chisels, nets, and tents being exchanged for meat and fur. In the early 1930s silver and uranium were discovered at what became Port Radium. By the 1950s, a church, a Hudson's Bay Store, a school, and a nursing station had all been built at Fort Franklin. During the fifties nearly all of the Bear Lake people settled relatively permanently at Fort Franklin, a site traditionally used as a meeting place and an important fishery. Settlement at Fort Franklin again restricted their socio-economic system and reduced, even more, the flexibility of their traditional subsistence pattern.

The reasons people give for moving into Fort Franklin vary. However, many people mention the availability of services provided by the church, schools, and the store as having been important. Of particular importance, apparently, was the school. People knew and were told that their children had to attend school. If a couple's children were not in school, that family could not receive pensions and assistance from the government. Faced with the choice of leaving their children at Fort Franklin during the year (thereby losing the companionship and support of their children in the bush), or settling at Fort Franklin, eventually all of the Bear Lake people chose the latter. Nowadays, when men go to the bush they normally leave behind their wives so that their children will be cared for. Also, during this period (the late 1940s and 1950s) the government conducted a massive tuberculosis eradication program which included sending many men and women 'outside' to Edmonton. This of course, confined many households to the settlement. Families couldn't or didn't want to go the bush without their relatives and when those relatives returned from the hospital, many couldn't work full-time on the land. No one can deny the need for this program of tuberculosis eradication, though it should be remembered that tuberculosis among the Dene resulted, in the first place, from contact with white people.

Whatever the immediate reasons people give for having settled at Franklin, it is apparent that the ultimate reasons, or causes, stem from forces outside of the traditional Bear Lake socio-cultural system. Settlement at Franklin was the result of technological, economic, social, and political pressures which accompanied contact with a dominant white society.

Since moving to Franklin the Bear Lake people have faced many changes in their way of life. Children have been educated in a white school system; English has been learned by many of the people; band and hamlet councils have been established; freight coming into Franklin has increased tremendously; a community co-op store has been organized; rental housing has been built; and wage-labour has increased. In spite of all these changes, most of which are in the material or technological realm, the Bear Lake people retain much of their traditional culture and most of their traditional values. When organizing their way of living, they rely, for the most part, upon their own cultural knowledge and their own values, not those of white society.

In the past, faced with the problem of making a living off their land, the Bear Lake people solved this problem by developing a particular kind of flexible social organization and mobile settlement pattern. By doing so, they were able to exploit very efficiently all of the animal resources available. But since 1950, the imposition of a new settlement pattern has undermined the ability of the Bear Lake people to find a happy socio-cultural solution to the problems of exploiting the fish and animal resources of their environment. Contact with a dominant white society established conditions which made it more difficult to live off the land and which, consequently, resulted in some reduced land use among the Great Bear Lake people. This is *not* to say, of course, that the Bear Lake people are not now utilizing the resources of their land, for they continue to derive an important part of their income from the land. Rather, it is that the new settlement pattern, introduced from the outside, has made it more difficult for them to use their land efficiently. If land use among these people is reduced, then the explanation of this fact resides in conditions *imposed* upon them from the outside.

The fact that, given permanent residence at Fort Franklin, it is now more difficult for the Bear Lake people to exploit their traditional animal and fish resources does not entail the conclusion that an economic system based upon Western industry and wage-labour must be established. What it does entail is the conclusion that new forms of technology and new kinds of work organization must be employed as new solutions to the problems of living off the land at Bear Lake. For example, since people no longer live on the North Shore and around Hottah Lake, it is more difficult, nowadays, for them to hunt barren-ground caribou than it was in the past. In response to this, new kinds of technology (e.g., snowmobiles, larger boats, and chartered aircraft) and new kinds of work groups (e.g., hunting groups organized by the Band Council and the Hamlet Trappers Association) have made it possible to continue to hunt for caribou. Recall the increase in participation by Bear Lake men in barren-ground caribou hunting during the period under consideration. In light of the extent to which governmental programs have undermined the efficient use of their land by the Bear Lake people, it is interesting to see an example of a program which, apparently, has had the opposite effect. Based upon this example, there seems to be no reason the Bear Lake people could not, if they so choose, develop a community-based economy founded substantially upon the continued use of traditional resources. The question is whether or not this alternative will continue to be available if demands and restraints continue to be imposed from outside.

Life in the bush

It is obvious that their land and a bush-oriented way of life mean much more to the Bear Lake people than can be expressed in Western dollar terms. By measuring the utility of traditional land-use activities in dollars only, one misses or obscures many of the 'subjective preferences' or values which the people associate with such activities. The Bear Lake people, of course, discuss the importance of the foods and materials which they take from the land. However, they also emphasize a number of other positive values which cannot be measured in dollars. Such values were learned by them from their ancestors and are considered by them to be constants in their cultural tradition. They highly value participation in a way of life which requires hard work and industriousness and which demands the constant acquisition of knowledge through experience on the land. Life in the bush is very difficult and there is always something which must be done in order to survive: food must be obtained, fires must be kept, clothing and shelter must be looked after, dogs must be fed, and boats, snowmobiles, and toboggans must be repaired. They enjoy such constant activity and give recognition to those people who are most industrious and successful on the land. The knowledge required by these people is considerable and can only be obtained by experience in the bush. 'The bush is a hard school.'

The Bear Lake people highly value the independence and self-reliance characteristic of life in the bush. In the bush everyone is 'his own boss' and is responsible only to his partners and family. In the bush people are not dependent upon others for their living. They are not dependent upon white men for jobs, for school, and for food. Things are not 'upside down' when Bear Lake people are on their land and any of them can obtain what they need to live.

The Bear Lake people highly value the generosity and mutual support which is associated with the bush. Though men are their own bosses and are free to make most of their decisions for themselves, they normally travel with partners, make decisions together, help one another in any way required, and share their take (except fur) between them so that no one is without. Such reciprocity is, of course, not limited to the bush (as anyone visiting Fort Franklin will quickly see), yet Bear Lake people associate it with life on their land and stress its importance within that context.

NOTE

The research upon which this paper is based was conducted during the period May 1974 to July 1975, during which time I lived among the Bear Lake people. The results of my field work are reported in full in my study 'Recent Land-Use by the Great Bear Lake Indians' (1976) done for the Indian Brotherhood of the NWT for submission to the Berger Inquiry. In the collection of data I was assisted by Malo Bewule, Fibbie Tatti, and Steve Iveson of the Indian Brotherhood; I greatly benefitted from discussion with them of all aspects of the study. The Band Council and the Dene of Fort Franklin cooperated fully; indeed, the study is as much theirs as mine. Ellen B. Basso, Keith H. Basso, Thomas McGuire, and William Hobson read and commented upon an earlier version of this paper; some of their comments have been incorporated.

The Dene Economy

Michael Asch

Just prior to the coming of the white man, the economy of the region of the Dene was characterized by the dominance of small self-sufficient groups of approximately twenty to thirty related persons called by anthropologists 'local groups.' In order to maintain themselves these groups relied on the harvesting of the many kinds of bush resources found in the region, including a wide variety of fish, small game animals, big game such as moose and woodland caribou, and a number of kinds of edible berries. As well, they relied on other products such as trees which were important in constructing shelters, in transportation, and as fuel.

Given the nature of the terrain and the distribution of resources in the region, it is most likely that the local groups camped in winter near the shores of the larger lakes which dominate the region. Here the small game and fish, which were the staples of the diet, could be found in most constant supply.

Within these encampments (or local groups) labour was organized along age and sex lines with men primarily responsible for hunting big game and setting fish nets and the women and children for the collection of small game. As well, women were responsible for making clothing from local resources such as moose hide and rabbit skins. The primary techniques used in collecting animal resources were snaring with babiche or sinew snares and entrapment. As well, moose and other big game animals were hunted with bow and arrow, club, or spear when crossing water or open country. Fish were taken using nets made of woven willow bast or caribou babiche. Given this type of technology, it is reasonable to conclude that most often large game capture required co-operative labour in hunting parties. Co-operation was also important for women's production tasks.

Transportation in the winter at this time relied primarily on human labour and was accomplished almost exclusively on foot. Yet, paradoxical as it may seem, this form of transportation resulted in more group travel than in the later period when dog power was used in transportation. The reason for this is simple: without dog teams it was easier to bring people to the game than the other way around. Hence, it would appear that in winter people moved around more than in later periods and, in fact, may have travelled throughout the region in search of game, returning only occasionally to the fish lake base camp when the situation demanded it.

In summer, people travelled primarily by shallow drafted canoes, sometimes made of moose hide. They would go to one of the major lakes where an encampment of perhaps two hundred persons would be formed, probably around the times of the fish runs. Then, before winter, the people would return again to their small local groups.

It would appear that within local groups bush resources were distributed on the basis of reciprocity or mutual sharing. Generally speaking all participated equally in the good fortune of the hunters and all suffered equally when their luck turned bad. Although the distribution system was basically informal, there was apparently some formality concerning the way in which certain animals were shared in that specific parts were reserved for the hunter and persons closely related to his or her immediate family. In this way, individual ability could be recognized, but not at the expense of the collective good. Thus, it was the whole membership of the local group and not each family or each individual that defined the self-sufficient unit.

There is little direct evidence in historical or archaeological sources about the circulation of goods between local groups during this period. The productive base of the region is not highly varied as to resources, but it is somewhat variable from year to year as to the actual distribution of these resources on the land. Hence, the primary problem of circulation probably concerned the creation of a balance in any one year between local groups which had resources surplus to their needs and those which did not have the minimum resources necessary for survival.

Theoretically, there are two ways in which this imbalance could be corrected. Either the surplus goods could be moved to the people in need, or people could move to areas in which local surpluses existed. Given the nature of the technology as well as the kinship system as reported by early travellers, it would appear that the latter solution was probably the case. Thus, it would seem that the principle of mutual sharing of resources was extended beyond the local group to include all groups in the region. This was done through a kinship and marriage system which linked all the people in the region into a single social unit and thus conveyed to all reciprocal rights and obligations concerning the use of resources in the region.

In terms of inter-regional or inter-tribal exchange, the little archaeological and historical evidence available indicates that trade between groups did occur; copper as well as implements of European manufacture are found in the region even prior to the arrival of the European traders. Nothing of the mechanisms of this type of trade is known, however.

The regional economy, then, in the late aboriginal period was a total economy both in terms of production and circulation of goods. The people of the region were themselves wholly responsible for their own survival. They achieved this end by organizing themselves into self-sufficient local groups within which production and distribution were collective activities. Given the potential variation of resources in local regions from year to year, on occasion local groups found themselves unable to maintain their self-sufficiency. At these times, they would join with other local groups lucky enough to be enjoying a surplus. Hence, the principle of co-operation and mutual sharing found within local groups was extended to all the people of the region.

The period of direct involvement with the fur trade began in the last decade of the eighteenth century. Although contact was established as the result of the competition between the Hudson's Bay Company and the Northwest Company for hegemony in the western trade, virtually none of the intense rivalry between the two trading companies was transferred to the region. Here the Northwest Company maintained hegemony in the fur trade until 1821 when, with the amalgamation of the two companies, the new Hudson's Bay Company came into ascendancy. As a result, none of the disruptions in native life which marked the period of competition in other parts of Canada appeared in the North and, indeed, from the time of contact until roughly 1870 when the Bay lost its monopoly in the fur trade throughout Rupert's Land, the fur trade was marked by stability.

During the period of HBC monopoly, the region was apparently considered too remote to command much attention. Bay policy required that remote posts such as those in the region remain self-sufficient in food provisions. Further, at least in the period from 1821 to 1850, Bay conservation policies inhibited trading in furs at all posts in North America including those in the region. As well, supply lines at this time were maintained through the use of York boats and brigading from Winnipeg to the West, imposing severe restrictions on the amount of goods and furs which could be transported to and from the North.

Given these transportation and trading restrictions, goods available for trade at remote posts were limited both in kind and quantity. Of the goods available, the most important for the Indians probably were the new staples such as flour, tea and sugar; metal utensils and implements; beads; blankets; tobacco and alcohol. In order to obtain these goods, the Indians had to trade local resources. Given the limitations of the goods and the policy restrictions mentioned above, it would appear that production for the fur trade was not great and consisted mainly of providing food provisions rather than furs.

From this evidence, it appears that the economy of the native people of the region changed little during this period from its aboriginal strategy. The economy of the region was still 'total' in that the people of the region, including both natives and Bay personnel, depended for their survival almost exclusively on local resources. For the native people production, despite the new utensils and implements, was still primarily a collective activity, and distribution of goods within and between local groups was still based on the principle of sharing. The only significant changes in native economic life during this time were the adoption of certain trade good items that made life a little easier and a shift in seasonal round to include both occasional trips to the trading posts for supplies at various times in the year, and, especially later in the period, the occasional use of the trading posts rather than the major lakes as places for encampment during the summer.

With the sale of Rupert's Land in 1870, the Hudson's Bay Company lost its monopoly in most of its former domain and with it an assured supply of furs at prices well below world market levels. In some areas of the Mackenzie region, such as Fort Wrigley and Fort Norman, monopoly conditions continued to obtain until as late as perhaps 1900. In other parts of the region, such as Fort Simpson and upstream, the operation of free traders further south was soon felt by the Bay. In order to meet this new competition, the Bay needed to provide more trade goods and provide them more cheaply. The major stumbling block to accomplishing this was the continued use of an outmoded transportation system which was costly, inefficient, and taxed to capacity. To solve this problem (perhaps spurred on by the development of an independent steam transport system by the Roman Catholic missionaries) the Bay reacted by replacing the York boats with steam, first on the Athabasca in 1882 and then on the Mackenzie in 1885, and by moving the major trans-shipment point to the North from Winnipeg to Edmonton after the completion of the rail link from Calgary to Edmonton in 1891. Between 1870 and 1890, transportation to the North was thus revolutionized from a system based on an eighteenth-century model to a modern one. Control by the Bay was seen to be in terms of virtual monopoly in transportation and retail sales, where it felt it could maintain a high level of profit.

The effects of competition and the new transportation system, as well as the Yukon gold rush of 1898 and the rise in fur prices during the First World War led to the complete transformation of the fur trade. To begin with there was a major change in the kinds and quantities of goods available. Among the new items now introduced were the repeating rifle, the steel trap, wide varieties of Western clothing, dogs and dog teams, and chocolates and other luxury items. As well, after the development of steam transportation, the numbers of traditional exchange items such as food staples, blankets, and metal utensils available in the North increased dramatically.

Second, a major shift occurred in trading power. Specifically, it is clear that the new transportation system, along with later improvements, created a condition in which the traders were no longer dependent upon local resources for survival, but rather could rely increasingly on external sources of provisions. This new-found independence of the fur traders had an effect on exchange relationships between the trader and the Indian. In order to obtain trade goods natives still traded local resources, but, whereas in the earlier period either provisions or furs could be used equally in exchange, now the Bay and the free traders alike could manipulate the exchange relationships to encourage trade in furs over food. Thus, for example, as early as 1871 the Bay limited the trade in percussion rifles to furs, though food (and furs) could be used to get less advanced guns. As well, late in the nineteenth century, the Bay changed its standard of trade by doubling the exchange value of furs to that of provisions. The process changing the economic relationship was capped in the 1890s by the introduction of money as the medium of exchange and the demise of the old barter system.

As a result of these externally initiated developments in the fur trade, the native economy of the region had shifted by 1900 in some areas, and by 1914 in all areas, from its virtual independence of trade goods to a situation where both trade goods and local subsistence resources were significant. Yet, the internal organization of the economy did not change greatly. The primary economic unit for most natives still remained the local group which, in most cases, still wintered at fish lakes. Further, labour was still organized on the basis of age and sex with the women and children responsible for collecting small game, and the men for hunting, fishing, and now trapping.

Some changes in production resulted from the introduction of the rifle and the steel trap. Of these, perhaps the most significant was the new-found ability of individuals to maintain more independence of others in their hunting and trapping pursuits. But aboriginal hunting techniques were still employed in collecting most game, including big game animals, and so co-operation remained a significant component of production.

As well, some changes occurred in the mobility of the people. The advent of the trapline, the year-round availability of provisions at trading posts, and the introduction of dog teams encouraged settlement to the extent that during the early twentieth century many families built permanent dwellings at fish lakes and along traplines. Further, in order to obtain supplies and trade furs, the men now made at least two trips to the trading posts during the winter seasons. Generally, these were at Christmas and at Easter. However, the women and children most often did not accompany the men to the posts but remained, as before, in the bush throughout the winter months. Finally, summer travel was probably expanded by the introduction of motors on canoes and skows. But the seasonal round now almost always included summer encampments at the trading posts rather than at the major lakes.

Despite the increased individualization in production and the introduction of money into the economy, distribution both within and between local groups remained based on the principle of mutual sharing. Thus, the main change in the distribution system of the region was the great increase in the amount of trade between the native people and the traders.

In summary, the regional economy was transformed by the new fur trade conditions from a 'total economy' to one which relied both on local subsistence and the use of externally produced goods exchanged for furs, but this shift appears to have created no major changes in the internal dynamics of production and circulation within the native economy.

Nonetheless, as a result of this economic shift, which required minimal changes in production and virtually no change in distribution, the standard of living was greatly raised. This must have made people feel quite wealthy. This rise in the standard of living, however, had an unexpected consequence: dependency. For now the stability and success of the economy was dependent in large measure on external economic conditions such as a high market price for furs in relation to trade good prices and the availability of productive surpluses in one aspect of local resources, furs. The latter problem was chronic and, indeed, after the influx of whites into the North during the 1920s, almost led to the collapse of the economy. On the other hand, the first problem appeared, on the surface at least, to be insignificant for fur prices and trade-good prices remained in a stable relationship for over thirty years, through two world wars and the Great Depression. Yet, ultimately, it was this factor and not fur production itself that led to the collapse of the fur trade economy when, beginning after the Second World War and lasting at least through the Korean War, there was a long depression in the value of furs and an unprecedented rise in the prices of trade goods.

In the years immediately following the World War, it was hoped that fur prices would soon rise again. In the meantime, most people, supported in part by the general introduction of family allowance and old age pension payments during the late 1940s, maintained their fur trade economy focus. But by the 1950s it became apparent that the fur economy would never return, at least without direct government intervention. The Territorial Council in January 1956 unanimously passed a resolution which stated, in part, 'Whereas the real income derived from fur trapping in the Northwest Territories is less than one-third of its pre-war level ... and whereas it is not possible for a person to live and to provide the minimum needs of his family at the present prices of fur ... [be it resolved that] the Commissioner be requested to ask the Minister of Northern Affairs and Natural Resources to request the Government of Canada most strongly to give immediate consideration to the provision of assistance to the people of the Northwest Territories through the establishment of an appropriate measure of support for the price of fur; or, alternatively, to take all possible measures at the earliest date to stimulate the economic development of the Northwest Territories so that alternative means of employment and income can be provided for these people.'

The Government acted by adopting a position basically in favour of economic development. To this end Jean Lesage, Minister of Northern Affairs and Natural Resources, proclaimed the 'New Education Programme' for the Northwest Territories which recommended the construction of school facilities in smaller centres and a program of hostel construction in larger ones to facilitate universal education. This solution was apparently approved of by at least some of the native chiefs, for it seemed a way for the youth to overcome the problems of the contemporary economic situation.

As a result of this policy, by the early 1960s grade schools had been constructed in virtually all the communities in the region and in most cases people were encouraged to move into town where they would continue to receive benefits and could remain with their children. For the others, it was pointed out that:

forgetful children should not forget that school is compulsory and that missing school for five consecutive or separate times is liable to punishment. Parents who fail to send their children to school without serious reason and notification to the teacher are liable to be fined and jailed. Moreover family allowance payments may be cancelled upon report made by the proper authorities. Mark well, children, that missing part of the day accounts for a day's absence, in so far as the punishments are concerned. Therefore, do your share for your sake and that of your family. (*The Catholic Voice*, 1957:5)

Given the economic conditions at the time, the threat of the loss of family allowances must have been quite an inducement to those unwilling to volunteer to send their children to school. In any event, voluntarily or not, most people, at least in the Fort Simpson and Fort Wrigley regions, moved into town within one year of the opening of a winter-term school.

The new circumstances had a profound effect on the internal organization of the regional economy. The movement of people away from residence at fish lake encampments and the introduction of direct family allowance payments, old age pensions, and other cash benefits directly to nuclear family heads and individuals, completely undermined the economic rationale of the local group. Thus, beginning no later than 1960, the nuclear family, typically composed of an older married couple and their adult and younger children, became the primary self-sufficient economic unit.

Further, while the over-all economy still relied on both bush resources and trade goods, with the demise of fur itself as the means for obtaining trade goods, the internal organization of the economy was forced to shift into two virtually independent spheres of production and distribution: one for bush subsistence, the other for trade good subsistence.

Concerning the former, production and distribution were little changed. Production was still organized as previously, but the move into town meant that the men, who for the most part still retained their fishlake hunting and trapping areas, had to travel long distances to obtain bush resources. On the other hand, the fact of permanently enlarged local populations meant the eventual depletion of the small game in the vicinity of the communities and thus, ultimately, the virtual abandonment of winter collection activities on the part of women.

Aside from the fact that the primary mutually sharing group shifted away from the local group, there was also little change in the ideology of distribution in the bush resource sector. Reciprocity still obtained in bush resource circulation both within the nuclear family and, where surpluses were available, between families that had once co-resided within a single local group. Indeed, in a few instances, bush resources were shared within the community as a whole, despite official counter-pressures against the ideology of reciprocity - for example, through government supervision of the distribution of game kept in community freezers.

Whereas in the past furs alone had had an exchange value sufficient to fill the trade good needs of the economy, now with the collapse of the fur trade, this was no longer the case. Thus, people needed to obtain cash in addition to the income received from trapping. In most cases, families relied upon direct cash payments from the government such as family allowances, old age pensions, and, in a few cases, welfare, to make up the difference. As well, in some families some or all of the cash needed to live was generated by part or full-time wage labour.

In terms of distribution, the cash–trade goods economic sector had an ideology which seemed to take on features both of white society and the traditional native one. On the one hand, the 'production,' that is the 'cash' itself, was not shared except to purchase those trade goods necessary to fill the needs of the nuclear family, and, indeed, any income generated by family members surplus to these was apparently considered as the private property of the income earner to be used either to purchase on an individual ownership basis personal consumer items such as portable radios, record players, musical instruments, and amplifiers; for personal travel; or, in some cases, to be buried away somewhere as a useless thing. In rare instances, surplus money was 'lent' (at no interest) to close relatives, but it was never shared. On the other hand, however, traditional trade goods, and especially food items, although now purchased with money rather than furs, were treated like bush resources and formed a significant part of the reciprocity system of distribution.

Finally, the movement into town also had a profound effect on mobility and travel. While it is true that in the fur trade period women and children remained fixed at fish lake encampments throughout the winter, they did travel extensively in summer. Now, however, aside from brief trips in the summer time, the women remained rooted throughout the year at the town-sites. Here they resided, initially in houses that had originally been intended only for summer use, and later, in some places, in government-built dwellings. Further, the winter round for the men had reversed itself in that rather than venturing from the bush into town a few times during the season to obtain trade goods, they now travelled from town to the bush a few times a year to obtain bush supplies. Finally, the younger children remained in the local communities for the whole year and then as they grew older went on to the major centres to continue their education. Thus, they often never experienced living throughout the winter in the bush.

It would seem, then, that the past thirty years has been an era of marked change in the internal organization of the economy, in that production and circulation in the spheres of bush subsistence and cash–trade good subsistence became virtually independent of each other. As well, government policies introduced during the past thirty years have themselves created fundamental changes in those aspects of economic organization pertaining to the size and composition of the self-sufficient economic units, mobility, and travel, and, perhaps most importantly, contact with the bush on the part of the younger generation.

It is clear that the contemporary native economy has not solved the problem of dependency on external agencies. Indeed, the problem has only deepened and become more obvious as direct government payments have replaced productive labour as the main resource for obtaining trade goods; these payments are seen by most people, native and non-native, as hand-outs to the poverty stricken.

Contemporary social and economic problems

A host of problems arise out of the relationship between native people and external agents. All are related to a single theme: that external agents introduce programs over which native people have no control and then force native people to co-operate with them. Of the many specific kinds of problems in this category, I would like to concentrate here on those related to welfare and wage labour.

The problem of welfare is not limited to the amount or pervasiveness of the payments themselves. Rather, it is importantly connected to the very form in which they are given, that is, to individual families. The traditional distribution system ensured that there was little wealth differentiation. This, as well, is true of the distribution system related to the bush subsistence sector of the economy today. On the other hand, the introduction of welfare payments, in their present form, created the individualization of poverty and helped to relieve the community of the traditional responsibility to help one another. This then led to the undermining of the values of collective responsibility which are part of the reciprocal economy and subtly led to the forced acceptance of the value of individual responsibility which is characteristic of our economy. In this sense, then, welfare represents a social intrusion that goes far beyond the mere question of dollars and cents, for it creates a perfidious influence on the native people to change their values.

The second problem area, wage labour, is closely related to the question of welfare. The introduction of permanent wage employment for only a small minority of people in the 1950s could have undermined the traditional value of economic equality by creating a class of rich and poor. However, during the 1950s and early 1960s, at least in Fort Wrigley, there was little temptation to spend large amounts of money as luxury consumer items were rather scarce. Since the jobs went to responsible family heads, the excess money was often used for socially useful activities such as supporting children attending schools in other communities, or was not used at all.

With the rapid development of the North in recent years and the concommitant rise in the amount of consumer goods available, this situation has changed. Now, there are many well-paying seasonal jobs especially in oil and gas exploration. Given the nature of these jobs, virtually all go to young men and, at least in Fort Wrigley, overwhelmingly to unmarried ones. Thus, wealth, in terms of purchasing power, has become concentrated in the hands of those with the fewest economic responsibilities. As a result, much of this income is expended on personal luxury items or on socially useless activities such as drinking parties. (Indeed, it would appear that to some extent the problem of alcohol abuse is generated by the excesses generated through wage labour.)

In addition, the fact that payment goes to individuals has helped to create a distinction between the rich young, who work for wages, and the seemingly poor young men, who collect bush resources for the family. And yet, given the ways in which most wage-generated income is spent, it is clearly the latter's activities which are socially more useful both to the individual family and to the community as a whole.

In short, in today's circumstances wage labour is often less of a solution than it is a problem - despite what the industry-sponsored studies say. On the one hand, it is acting as a subtle influence to change values away from mutual sharing and towards individualistic ones. On the other, it is concentrating wealth in the hands of those who are least capable or willing to use it in socially useful ways, while at the same time helping to undermine the respect for others who perform socially more valuable labour.

The common theme which connects these and other problems is that they are in large measure the result of the intrusion of southern institutions and values into the on-going processes of native life. As a result of this social and economic domination, native people in the last twenty years have been under ever-increasing pressure to abandon their traditional way of life and replace it with institutions and values like those of the south. Yet, despite conscious and unconscious efforts to effect this end, this process has not been completely successful and, indeed, many aspects of the traditional way of life survive and even flourish.

Native people are not succumbing, but rather are working to solve these problems which face them and regain control over their own lives.

This response dates back at least as far as the first intrusion into native political autonomy at the time of the so-called treaty signings. However, it has only been in recent years, with the rise of territorial-wide political organizations such as the Indian Brotherhood of the Northwest Territories and the Metis Association, that the response has generated political power. This culminated in the land claim and the Dene Declaration through which, it is hoped, the native people will be able to regain control over their economic, political, and social institutions.

The land claim is not a problem, as industry-sponsored studies suggest, but an attempt to find a solution to a range of problems. It is ironic but significant that among the strongest supporters of the land claim are the young and well-educated - the very individuals the industry-sponsored studies suggest are the most alienated from the traditional way of life and the most willing to embrace the western one.

In reading the testimony at the community hearings of the Pipeline Inquiry and in talking with the young men of Wrigley myself, I find an overwhelming majority who do not want to abandon their traditional life style and see the land claim settlement as a way to protect themselves in future from what has happened to their society without such protection in the past. The important point is that they are not sitting around waiting for the south to solve their problems for them but have arrived at a proposed direction for a solution themselves. The question is whether or not they will be allowed to take that path and make it work.

On a local level, the adoption of a co-op in Fort Wrigley has also been an attempt to seek a solution to some of their problems. The co-op is run by a board of directors composed entirely of native people. It is operated in such a way that many jobs are provided on a part-time basis and preference is often given to heads of families. This organization, of course, provides equity in the distribution of income, ensures that money goes to responsible individuals, and enables people to spend time pursuing bush-collection activities. It is, to say the least, a more appropriate form of wage employment than that used by the business community. It further shows that where local people have some control over their internal organization of economic institutions, they can make them run in such a way as to maintain traditional values such as mutual sharing even in the cash sector of the economy.

There are, as well, other examples of the people of Fort Wrigley working to solve their own problems. These range from the collective resistance to the Mackenzie Highway to the formation of community-wide organizations such as the health and the women's committees.

Conclusion

I have attempted to demonstrate that the problems faced by native people today stem from two fundamental themes. These are:
1 that the genesis of many problems for native people was the fact that, unbeknownst to them, their relationship with the fur trade in the period after 1870 created an exchange in which they received immediate material well-being in return for economic dependency on outside agents: a dependency that became real after the collapse of the fur trade and which has been maintained through post-war government intervention. And
2 that most of the problems facing northern natives today arise as the result of the intrusion of southern institutions and values into the on-going processes of Dene life, especially in the post-war 'depression' years.

The Dene have proposed a solution to these problems in the form of a land settlement which, if it follows the principles of the Dene Declaration, will enable them to regain control over their economic, social, and political institutions. I agree with this position, for I am convinced that without such control the process of intrusion will continue and will ultimately erode the viability of their institutions and their livelihoods.

How then does the proposed gas pipeline and attendant development relate to these concerns? Let me begin with the question of dependency. To my mind, the proposals regarding this development are strikingly similar to the bargain proposed by the fur traders about a hundred years ago: that is, immediate material well-being in return for long-term economic dependency. But in one respect this new bargain is quite different: whereas the fur trade deal created maximum material benefit for native people with minimal changes in their traditional economic activities and organization, this new one requires as a precondition for participation the acquisition of certain specialized skills necessary to obtain employment. Furthermore, it implies another but more subtle change. The pipeline applicants anticipate the further erosion of the self-sufficient bush collection sector of the economy in favour of even more dependence on the cash-trade goods sector; the means by which this will be accomplished is the desire of young native men to have the relative 'security' of wage employment.

Whether or not wage employment is secure anywhere in Canada given our economic system is a moot question. What is of specific concern, however, is that there is no guarantee that employment in the petroleum industry will be secure in the North over a long period. Just as the fur trade's viability depended upon the availability of furs and a high world market price for them, so does the viability of petroleum development depend on the availability of oil and a high world market price for it. But what happens, for example, when the resource gives out, or if we in the south find a cheaper source of fuel in the next decade or so? What happens if the world market price of petroleum products declines to a point where it is uneconomic to exploit and transmit northern oil and gas to southern markets? The answer is obvious. The petroleum corporations, just like the fur traders before them, will pull out. I do not intend this statement to imply criticism of their motives. This is, after all, the way the system works. Their objective is not, and should not be, to help native people; it is to sell oil and gas at a profit. Therefore, they must leave if the proposition becomes uneconomic and, of course, that day inevitably will come.

But what will happen to native northerners when this does occur? If we follow the history of the fur trade, the answer is known: there will be a general collapse in the cash-trade goods sector of the economy. If we follow the projections of the industry-sponsored studies this collapse will be much more severe than that created by the fur trade dependency. They suggest that within the next decade, first the economy of the native people will have been transformed from its present situation in which there are two viable but independent sectors (one concerned with bush resource collection and the other with cash-trade goods subsistence) to one which is almost totally dependent upon the cash-trade goods sector; and second, that a large segment of the native community will consist of a highly trained labour force specializing in petroleum exploration and related activities, a group unwilling or unable to use the bush as a means of obtaining subsistence.

Hence there is a very real possibility that should the collapse occur after the next decade it would be too late to recover the traditional economic way of life and the result would therefore be the transformation of the northern native people into the general class of southern Canadian 'poor.'

Thus, the bargain the petroleum corporations are proposing to the native people is as follows: 'In return for reorganizing your labour force to suit our needs, we will provide you with employment for an indefinite period of time. As a result of our high wages, your people may well stop pursuing their traditional bush collection activities and therefore when we leave, as inevitably we must, there is a good possibility that you will be unable to sustain yourselves in your native land.' It is against this type of proposition that native people must protect themselves.

Yet, as the history of the fur trade shows, merely being participants in development will not accomplish this end. What is necessary is that native people have effective control over northern development. Only then can they decide which developments are in their own interest, and provide safeguards to ensure that those aspects of their traditional economy, including bush resource collection activities that they wish to maintain, remain viable. A land settlement, should it follow the principles of the Dene Declaration, will provide this type of control and therefore should be supported.

The contemporary period has not been the most pleasant for native people or a particularly ennobling one for southern Canadian society in its dealings with northern natives. Indeed, in the past thirty years southern Canadian society, perhaps with all the best intentions, has done more to undermine the institutions and values of native society than in the previous one hundred years. Yet, despite our intrusions into virtually every facet of native society, traditional economic, social, and political institutions and values persist and, in some cases, flourish. Furthermore, the Dene have not only coped with this massive intrusion, but have responded to the situation by working to solve the problems which we have presented them. As well, they have proposed through their land claim a general solution to these problems. Should a permit to begin construction of a pipeline be granted prior to a land settlement and the informed consent of the native northerners, it will definitely undermine their attempts to regain control over the direction of their society, for the single largest decision about their future will have been made without their approval. Thus, the granting of a permit prior to a land settlement will only exacerbate the present situation and undermine the initiatives native people have undertaken to solve their problems.

In conclusion, I fully support the position of the native people that there must be 'no pipeline before a land settlement.' Indeed, to my mind, it is the only reasonable protection that the Dene can receive to safeguard themselves against the complexity of problems both already known and as yet unanticipated that must inevitably accompany a development scheme of this magnitude.

NOTE

This paper draws on my historical research on the Slavey Indians in the area east of the Mackenzie River between Fort Simpson and Fort Norman, and my field work in the Slavey community of Fort Wrigley. My conclusions should generally apply in the whole Dene region.

The Loss of Economic Rents

Arvin D. Jelliss

In its 1975 *Discussion Paper on Northern Development* the Science Council of Canada posed the following fundamental question: 'In whose economic interest should the North be developed?' The problems faced by the native people of the North suggest an immediate answer: any development that occurs should first of all benefit the native people by contributing in a significant way to their development efforts.

Because the development objectives of the native people are of a long-term nature, the most important way in which natural resources projects can contribute to these objectives is related to the economic rents associated with these projects. As the southern provinces of Canada and an increasing number of the less developed countries have come to realize during the last few years, the major long-term benefits that flow from natural resources projects have to do with the appropriation and subsequent utilization of these economic rents. Who receives these rents, and the uses to which they are put, are therefore important areas of study.

A major point at issue in the case of the proposed Mackenzie Valley gas pipeline is the extent to which the native peoples of the Northwest Territories would benefit from its construction and operation. Since the proposed pipeline would presumably operate, in the absence of a negotiated land settlement, under institutional arrangements similar to those that have governed previous natural resources projects, a consideration of the distribution of the economic rents associated with their activities is in order. Such an analysis will allow us to see to whom the existing institutional arrangements have directed the long-term benefits associated with past natural resources projects in the Northwest Territories, and hence to whom they are most likely to direct those relating to future projects.

Natural resources projects in the Northwest Territories since 1970 are here examined from this perspective. Estimates of the magnitude and distribution of the economic rents associated with their activities are presented, explanations for the observed structures of rent distribution are advanced, and the implications of this evidence for the relationship between natural resources projects and native people's development in the Northwest Territories are discussed. The Pointed Mountain natural gas project is considered in greater detail.

Economic rent

The economic rent associated with a natural resources project may be defined as the revenue accruing to the project after the deduction of all costs of production, including an adequate return to invested capital. In the southern provinces of Canada during the last few years a number of rent-collection arrangements have been instituted which have resulted in the people of those provinces obtaining a greater share of this economic rent. In the Northwest Territories, on the other hand, because the rights of the native people as landowners have not been recognized, the rents accruing to natural resources projects have been divided between the operating companies, in the form of excess profits (i.e., profits over and above an adequate return to invested capital), and the federal government, in the form of taxes and royalties. None of these rents have accrued to the native people for use in pursuing their own development objectives.

A further problem has been that, in some cases, not all of the potential revenue associated with the production and subsequent sale of a resource has flowed through to the project. Pointed Mountain natural gas, for example, not only is sold at less than its competitive energy value vis-à-vis alternative fuels at the Canada–United States border but at least until 1975 all the border price increases that did occur accrued in the first instance to the transmission company in British Columbia, instead of to the producer in the Northwest Territories. This means that both United States consumers of Pointed Mountain natural gas, as well as certain entities in British Columbia, have received a portion of the economic rent associated with the Pointed Mountain project – United States consumers in the form of undervalued gas prices, and entities in British Columbia in the form of excess transmission charges. As the Pointed Mountain example illustrates, it is not always appropriate simply to consider the revenues accruing to the producer when estimating the economic rent associated with a particular natural resources project.

The rent estimates in this paper show the actual or potential revenue accruing to a natural resources project after the deduction of all costs of production, including a 15 per cent return to invested capital. The rent and rent distribution estimates relate to the years 1970-74 inclusive. They have been adjusted to allow for inflation and are expressed in 1975 dollars. They have been converted to 1975 present values by compounding at 10 per cent. (The detailed computations on which they are based may be found in my research studies done for the Indian Brotherhood of the NWT).

Mining

Between 1970 and 1974 six mining projects were at work in the Northwest Territories. The Pine Point lead-zinc mine and Con/Rycon gold mines are both majority-owned and controlled by Cominco, which is in turn majority-owned and controlled by Canadian Pacific Investments, Ltd. Canadian Pacific itself participates in the Arctic Gas consortium through its ownership interest in Trans Canada Pipelines. The Giant Yellowknife gold mine is 19 per cent owned by Falconbridge Nickel Mines, which is in turn controlled by the Superior Oil Company of the United States through its ownership interest in McIntyre Mines Ltd. The Canada Tungsten mine is 42 per cent owned by American Metal Climax Incorporated. The Echo Bay silver mine is owned by the International Utilities Corporation of Philadelphia.

An analysis of the rents associated with the activities of these mines between the beginning of 1970 and the end of 1974 revealed that the present value (in 1975) of these past rents amounted to $195 million, and that of this total, the mining companies retained $102.5 million, or 52.6 per cent, in the form of excess profit, while the federal government received $77.4 million, or 39.6 per cent, from taxes, and $15.1 million, or 7.8 per cent, from royalties.

This structure of rent distribution is basically the result of the federal government's royalty and taxation policies as they apply to natural resources projects in the Northwest Territories. Within this structure, apart from the share of the rent taken by taxation, the companies retain over 85 per cent in the form of excess profits because of rather generous royalty arrangements. In the southern provinces, by contrast, a much smaller share of federal-tax-exclusive rents would accrue to the companies, because provincial mining taxes and royalty arrangements would appropriate a greater share for the benefit of the people.

The rents retained by the companies are presumably either paid out in the form of dividends to shareholders, or are used to finance investments which enhance the long-term viability and profitability of corporate operations. The location of these new investments may be in Canada, the United States, or in any country in which the ultimate rent recipients perceive their long-term interests to lie.

Consider the activities of Cominco, which owns 69 per cent of the Pine Point mine, 100 per cent of the Con mine, and 76 per cent of the Rycon mine. During the 1970-74 period these mines between them collected $75.3 million in rents from their activities in the Northwest Territories. This represents almost three-quarters of all company-retained rents from mining projects in the Northwest Territories during these years. On the basis of its ownership interests in these mines the bulk of these rents would have accrued to Cominco. A portion of these rents may have been retained at the mine, another portion paid out to Cominco's shareholders (of which Canadian Pacific Investments Ltd. would have received 54 per cent), and the rest used to help finance investments contributing to the long-term viability and profitability of the corporation.

During 1970-74, for example, Cominco was engaged in reopening the H.B. lead and zinc mine near Salmo in British Columbia, in opening the Black Angel mine in western Greenland, in gaining an Australian base of operations by acquiring a 55 per cent interest in Aberfoyle Ltd., and in rehabilitating the Vade potash mine in Saskatchewan. At the present time Cominco is engaged in constructing a new ammonia-urea complex near Carseland, Alberta, at an estimated cost of $130 million. Its current exploration projects are concerned with diamonds in the Central African Republic, copper-molybdenum in Mexico, zinc in Kentucky, oil and gas in Texas and New Mexico, lead-zinc-copper-silver in Tasmania, and, somewhat closer to home, lead-zinc and uranium in the Northwest Territories.

While these activities presumably reveal a corporate long-term strategy, they quite obviously have little to do with solving the development problems of the native people in the Northwest Territories. At the same time as the economic rents associated with Cominco's current mining projects in the Northwest Territories contribute to the viability and profitability of its long-term operations, they fail to contribute in any meaningful way to the long-term development objectives of the native people. The reason is quite straightforward: the institutional arrangements governing natural resources projects in the Northwest Territories provide no mechanism by which the inhabitants can obtain a share of the economic rents associated with their activities.

Crude oil production at Norman Wells

Production of crude oil at Norman Wells dates from 1921, and is conducted by Imperial Oil Ltd., 69 per cent owned and controlled by the Exxon Corporation, formerly the Standard Oil Company (New Jersey).

An analysis of the rents associated with Norman Wells crude oil production between the beginning of 1970 and the end of 1974 revealed that the present value in 1975 of these past rents amounted to $34.5 million, and that of this total, consumers of Norman Wells products received $25.4 million, or 73.6 per cent, in the form of lower prices, the federal government received $5.4 million, or 15.8 per cent, in the forms of a share of net revenue, taxes, and royalties, and Imperial Oil received $3.7 million, or 10.6 per cent, in the form of excess profits. The reasons for this structure of rent distribution relate to both the federal government/Imperial Oil financial relationships for the operation at Norman Wells and to the federal government's local and national pricing policies.

The revenue-sharing arrangement negotiated between the federal government and Imperial Oil regarding Norman Wells crude oil production results in the federal government's receiving (a) one-third of the net value of natural gas and crude oil production, plus (b) a 5 per cent royalty on the gross value of the remaining two-thirds, minus (c) an Imperial Oil management fee calculated as 10 per cent of the federal government's share of production and development costs. In return, Imperial Oil is allowed to expense all development expenditures as they occur, instead of having to apply the standard write-off procedures.

The price of Norman Wells refined products is apparently regulated by the federal government in such a way that the value of crude oil production is undervalued relative to the Alberta wellhead price plus the transportation costs of moving Alberta oil to Norman Wells. For example, in 1974 Norman Wells crude oil was valued at $3.32/barrel, whereas the Western Canada average was $5.72/barrel. If transportation costs were $1/barrel, Norman Wells crude oil was undervalued in 1974 by $3.40/barrel.

In addition to this, federal government policy with respect to the pricing of Canadian crude oil in general results in an undervaluation of the Alberta wellhead price relative to the world oil price. In 1974 the world oil price was around $11/barrel. The Western Canada average was, as we have seen, $5.72/ barrel, resulting in an undervaluation of the Alberta wellhead price relative to the world price of $5.28/barrel. Adding this to the undervaluation previously derived results in an undervaluation of Norman Wells crude oil in 1974 of $8.68/barrel.

Although the information currently available does not allow an exact identification of who receives the consumer rent, there are some indicators. In 1974 the anticipated sales value of refined products at Norman Wells was estimated at just over $6 million. Of this total, diesel fuel oil accounted for 41.3 per cent and aviation turbo fuel for 33 per cent. It would therefore seem that the major share of the rents associated with Norman Wells crude oil production accrue to the corporate sector – the companies attempting to 'develop' the Mackenzie Valley.

Natural gas production at Pointed Mountain

Pointed Mountain is the only producing gas field in the Northwest Territories. Production began in August 1972, conducted by Amoco Canada Petroleum

Company Ltd., a wholly owned subsidiary of Standard Oil Company (Indiana).

An analysis of the rents associated with the Pointed Mountain project between the commencement of production and the end of 1974 revealed the present value in 1975 of these past rents to amount to $66.3 million, of which United States consumers received $50.7 million or 76.5 per cent, in the form of undervalued gas prices, Canadian entities in British Columbia received $15 million, or 22.7 per cent, in the form of excess transmission charges, and the federal government received $0.6 million, or 0.8 per cent from royalties. The reasons for this rather disconcerting structure of rent distribution relate to both the sales arrangements respecting Pointed Mountain natural gas, and to the federal government's export pricing policy.

The sales contract between Amoco and Westcoast Transmission specified an initial price of 11.5¢ per thousand cubic feet of Pointed Mountain gas. Although the border export price of Canadian gas increased between August 1972 and December 1974 from 32¢ to $1 per thousand cubic feet, the price received by Amoco appears to have remained at 11.5¢. This means that entities in British Columbia (with the main candidates being Westcoast Transmission and the provincial government) were receiving a share of the rents associated with Pointed Mountain gas production.

At the same time, the contract under which Westcoast Transmission sold Pointed Mountain gas to its US customer grossly undervalued this gas in terms of its competitive energy value vis-à-vis alternative fuels. In August 1972, for example, the competitive energy value of Canadian gas at the US border was around 58¢ per thousand cubic feet, while the actual border price was 32¢. By December 1974, the actual border price had increased to $1. However, a National Energy Board study published the previous July had indicated that the competitive energy value of Canadian gas exported at Huntington, British Columbia (the export point for Pointed Mountain gas) was $1.57 by March of that year.

This combination of institutional arrangements resulted in over 75 per cent of the economic rents associated with the Pointed Mountain project accruing to US residents, while most of the remainder accrued to Canadian entities in British Columbia.

The total value of the rents associated with natural resources projects in the Northwest Territories between 1970 and 1974 approximated $296 million. Of this total, the operating companies retained $106 million (35.9 per cent) in the form of excess profits, i.e., profits over and above a 15 per cent return on their invested capital; the federal government received $98 million (33.8 per cent) mainly from taxes, but also from royalties and a share of Norman

Wells production revenue; entities in British Columbia received $15 million
(5.1 per cent) in the form of excess transmission charges on Pointed Mountain natural gas; Canadian (mainly corporate) consumers received $25 million
(8.6 per cent) in the form of lower prices for Norman Wells refined products;
and US consumers received $51 million (17.1 per cent) in the form of under-
valued natural gas prices.

A case study of the Pointed Mountain natural gas project

The native people of the Northwest Territories are faced with serious development problems. The native economy is characterized by low income per capita, a high dependence on welfare and other transfer payments, skills unsuited
to the demands of the high income sectors, the need to improve productivity
in traditional activities, and the lack of investment capital. The development
problem is further exacerbated by the lack of any significant decision-making
authority in strategic areas of interest such as land use. For all intents and
purposes, this resides with the federal government in Ottawa.

The main impetus to increased economic activity in the NWT derives from
the natural resources sector. It is therefore important to be able to assess the
extent to which this sector may be able to contribute to native people's development. On the basis of such an assessment, a set of institutional arrangements may be devised which will allow this contribution to be most effectively provided.

I would like to use the Pointed Mountain natural gas project as a case
study for such an assessment. This is the only exploited gas field in the NWT
and is located in the extreme southwest corner near the BC and Yukon borders.

In general, the contributions that a natural resources project may make to
the development process may be classified into direct and fiscal aspects.
Direct contributions may be divided into demand and supply side effects. On
the demand side, the projects demand for labour, materials, and equipment
may be satisfied from supply sources within the developing economy. The ex-
pansion of markets and incomes so induced may then lead, via linkage and
multiplier effects, to increased activity in less connected sectors of the economy.

On the supply side, the project may result in a new or lower-cost input
available for use in other sectors, or as a basis for the setting up of downstream processing activities. At the same time, the labour employed on the
project may accumulate new or improved skills, which are then available for
utilization elsewhere in the economy at a later date.

The fiscal contributions a natural resources project may make to a developing economy relate to the magnitude and subsequent utilization of the

government-appropriated portion of revenues accruing to the project after production commences. On the basis of its tax- and royalty-levying authority, a government may appropriate a portion of the revenues accruing to the project during the production stage. These revenues may then be used to provide infrastructural facilities, with the object of stimulating activity in the non-government sector. Alternatively, or in addition, they may be channelled into the non-government sector via loans or grants for private investment purposes.

Within this analytical framework, a consideration of the Pointed Mountain project is most usefully approached by distinguishing between its construction and early production phases. The construction phase of the project extended from late spring 1971 to October 1972, with major construction activity occurring during the early months of 1972. Three major facilities were constructed: a gas dehydration plant and associated gas gathering system at the Pointed Mountain field, and a transmission pipeline from Pointed Mountain to Beaver River in Northern British Columbia. The two Pointed Mountain facilities were the responsibility of the producer, Amoco Canada Petroleum Company Limited. The transmission pipeline was the responsibility of Westcoast Transmission Company Limited, and was designed to feed Pointed Mountain gas into the main Westcoast system for subsequent processing and distribution in British Columbia and the United States Pacific Northwest.

The direct impact of the construction phase of the project on the native economy may be summarized in the following way. On the demand side, since all materials and equipment were purchased in the south, there were no income linkage or multiplier effects associated with these expenditures in the NWT. With regard to the demand for labour, a 1973 federal government study, *The Socio-Economic Impact of the Pointed Mountain Gas Field* by M. Scott, estimated that a total of between 65 and 70 different native workers were employed on the project at one time or another during the construction period. Peak native employment on the project coincided with peak total employment towards the end of February 1972. At that time, of a total work force of 465 men, native employment reached 60 persons, or 12.9 per cent of the total. In general, native employment was intermittent and of relatively short duration. Native workers from the settlements of Fort Liard and Fort Simpson were estimated to have worked an average of 12.4 and 4.6 weeks, respectively, during the construction period.

Using sample data, Scott also estimated total native income from the project by settlement as between $50,000 and $75,000 for Fort Liard, approximately $40,000 for Fort Simpson, and between $6,000 and $10,000 for Nahanni Butte. This may be compared with total construction phase outlays amounting to approximately $15 million, implying a native economy content of construction period investment expenditures of between 0.64 per cent and 0.83 per cent. Further, there were little, if any, multiplier effects resulting from the wage component of construction expenditures. Contacts between project personnel and the nearest native settlement at Fort Liard were minimal. Native incomes derived from the project were spent mainly at settlement stores, all of which are owned in and derive their supplies from the south.

On the supply side, over 90 per cent of the jobs held by native people were in the unskilled category, with the main employment activities being clearing, brushing, and grading. Skill accumulation was therefore of a very limited magnitude.

The direct impact of the early production phase of the project on the native economy may be summarized briefly. Potential demand side-effects have been essentially restricted to the eight permanent positions available, of which half are categorized as skilled. However, all of these positions are held by southern Canadian personnel, and these men have little or no contact with the native economy.

On the supply side, no new or lower-cost inputs have been made available to the native economy. The cost of constructing a gas supply system to the community at Fort Liard has been estimated at $500,000 and could not be justified on the basis of estimated field life and market size. The possibility of this community being supplied with electricity generated at the project has been discussed, but no action has materialized.

Under the institutional arrangements governing natural resources projects in the NWT at the present time, there exist no mechanisms by which the native peoples may obtain any fiscal or fiscal-type benefits after production commences. Nevertheless, an analysis of the fiscal aspects of the Pointed Mountain project is important for at least two interrelated reasons. In the first place, as the evidence just presented has indicated, because of the extremely limited magnitude of direct benefits, any significant developmental contribution to the native economy from this project would have had to accrue through a fiscal-type mechanism. Secondly, given this fact, it is useful to identify to whom existing institutional arrangements have directed the potential fiscal-type benefits associated with the project. A basis is then provided from which a discussion of alternative institutional arrangements may proceed.

It is at this stage that the economic rent information takes on added significance. The present value, in 1975, of the economic rents from the Pointed Mountain project during the years 1972-74 was estimated at $66.3 million. This figure may be regarded as the potential fiscal or fiscal-type contribution that the project could have made to the native economy during these years. It also provides a basis from which to assess the adequacy of existing federal government rent-collection. (To repeat: up to the end of 1974 these arrangements had appropriated a mere \$0.6 million, or 0.8 per cent of the total rents associated with the project. At the same time, entities in British Columbia had received \$15 million, or 22.7 per cent, of those rents, while US consumers had received over \$50 million, or about 76 per cent, in the form of undervalued natural gas prices.)

This distribution of the economic rents associated with the early production phase of the Pointed Mountain project emphasizes both the inadequacy of existing federal government rent-collection mechanisms, and the inappropriateness of the existing institutional arrangements governing natural resources project in the NWT. Any institutional arrangements which direct over three-quarters of the economic rents associated with a natural resources project to foreign consumers, while at the same time appropriating less than 1 per cent via their rent-collection mechanisms, is quite obviously in need of a substantial overhaul. And when these rents are at the same time being directed away from the native peoples from whose land the resource is being extracted, and who have derived few other benefits from the project, it is not unreasonable to conclude that substantial institutional changes are in order.

What institutional arrangements would have been required in the case of the Pointed Mountain project? The Dene have appraised the relationship between natural resources projects and their development aspirations in the following way: 'We are saying that when developments do take place, and many already have, Indian people are entitled as owners of the land to receive revenues, or royalties. These royalties could then be put to work to create community enterprises. That way we could create a long-term economic base under Indian control and native people would be free of dependence on the Government and the developers to create jobs.' The Dene emphasize the fiscal-type contributions that natural resources projects can make to their development. They do not see increased wage employment as either a necessary or a sufficient ingredient in their long-term plans. Instead they see the economic rents associated with natural resources projects as being able to provide the investment funds required to develop native-controlled community enterprises.

Given the nature of the native people's development aspirations, the institutional arrangements governing natural resources projects in the NWT need to emphasize the appropriation, and subsequent utilization within the native economy, of the economic rents associated with such projects. The implementation of such arrangements in the case of the Pointed Mountain natural gas project would have implied the federal government's pursuit of two particular policy goals. The first of these would have been to ensure that the full value of economic rents associated with the projects flowed through to the NWT, instead of being dissipated to southern Canadian and US entities. More specifically, it would have required decisive action by the federal government to bring the Canadian export price of natural gas into line with its competitive energy value at the Canadian/United States border, and a similar decisiveness to ensure that this value, net of Westcoast processing and transmission costs, flowed through to the NWT.

The second policy requirement would have entailed the design and implementation of an efficient rent-collection mechanism in the NWT, which would have appropriated the increased revenues accruing to the project for subsequent use in the native economy. Further, the magnitude of the rents associated with the project indicate that this could not have been achieved by some marginal change in existing royalty schedules. Rather, it would have required the implementation of a significantly different rent-collection system, able to capture the full value of the economic rents associated with the project, and capable of channelling these rents into the native economy for investment in native-controlled community enterprises.

The federal government's failure to pursue either of these policy goals in a decisive way resulted in over 76 per cent of the economic rents associated with the Pointed Mountain project accruing to US consumers, while the native peoples of the NWT, faced with serious development problems, received none.

Thus the native peoples do not appear to be able to rely on the federal government adequately to represent their interests in this endeavour.

This conclusion may be substantiated by considering some further aspects of the Pointed Mountain gas project. In his introductory remarks before the House of Commons Standing Committee on Indian Affairs and Northern Development in March 1972, prior to the statement of the government's *Northern Objectives, Priorities and Strategies for the 70's*, the then Minister of Indian Affairs and Northern Development, Jean Chrétien, stated:

Fundamental to the Government's statement is our belief that native northerners should derive early, visible, and lasting benefits from economic development. Our efforts must not only be turned to developing the natural resources of the North for the benefit of Canada as a whole. The development of northern resources must first improve the standard of living and the well-being of northern residents. All too often the economic activity of the past was at their expense.

Construction relating to the Pointed Mountain project was already underway. Edgar Dosman in *The National Interest* indicates that this policy statement had been approved by the cabinet in July 1971, prior to any significant construction activity. Further, a report submitted to Westcoast Transmission by

Shultz International Limited, entitled *Ecological and Economical Impact of the Pointed Mountain Natural Gas Line*, and available to the federal government by September 1971, had already assessed the likely distribution of the economic benefits associated with the project. After noting that benefits during the construction phase in terms of equipment purchases and personnel requirements would accrue to British Columbia, Alberta, and other southern provinces receiving the appropriate contracts, the report went on to analyse the longer-term benefits in the following way:

Generally, the benefits of the proposed pipeline will be to the nation as a whole, as a result of the export of gas to the United States and the corresponding foreign exchange inflow which will result. The national economy will also benefit to the extent that Westcoast's profits will be distributed to Canadian shareholders ... Further, the net value of economic activity generated, both directly and indirectly through the multiplier, will benefit Canada as a whole.

We have, then, a situation where the cabinet approved a policy statement in which it is emphasized that natural resources projects not only should benefit Canada as a whole, but should result first in 'early, visible, and lasting benefits' to the native people, and on the other hand an evaluation stating that the Pointed Mountain project would confer no such benefits at all. One would naturally conclude that under these circumstances the federal government would not approve the project unless or until it had altered the institutional arrangements governing the project so that the native people would benefit. In fact, exactly the opposite occurred. The federal government approved the Pointed Mountain project by granting a right of way to Westcoast Transmission in November 1971. It then released its public policy statement to the House Standing Committee in March 1972, with construction well underway

The conclusion that must be drawn from any objective consideration of this evidence is clear. The native people cannot rely on the federal government alone to represent their interests in the case of proposed natural resources projects in the Northwest Territories.

The proposed Mackenzie Valley natural gas pipeline, if it is operated within the same institutional structure, will produce similar results – no local benefits from the rent created by the enterprise. To prevent this gross misallocation of benefits, fundamental changes in the institutional arrangements for natural resources development must first be implemented. The federal government has proved itself unable or unwilling to represent the interests of the native people. The position of the native people is that there should be no pipeline before a negotiated land claims settlement. Whatever the other merits of this position, the evidence presented here indicates it makes sound economic sense.

REFERENCES

Edgar J. Dosman, *The National Interest: The Politics of Northern Development 1968-75* (Toronto, 1975)

Jelliss, Arvin D., 'Estimates of Past and Future Rents and Rent Distribution Associated with Currently Operating Mines in the Northwest Territories' (Yellowknife: IBNWT, mimeo, Aug. 1975)

- 'Estimates of Past and Future Rents and Rent Distribution Associated with the Production of Gas at Pointed Mountain, Northwest Territories' (Yellowknife: IBNWT, mimeo, Dec. 1975)

- 'Estimates of Past and Future Rents and Rent Distribution Associated with the Production of Oil at Norman Wells, Northwest Territories' (Yellowknife: IBNWT, mimeo, Dec. 1975)

National Energy Board, *Report to the Governor in Council in the Matter of the Pricing of Natural Gas Being Exported Under Existing Licences* (Ottawa, 1974)

The Distribution of Economic Benefits from a Pipeline

John F. Helliwell

I have been involved for several years in research efforts designed to place Arctic energy developments in the broader context of Canadian energy supply and requirements. This has involved two main strands of research: one focused on the aggregate or macroeconomic effects of construction and operation of large energy projects, and the second concerned with the size and distribution of the economic costs and benefits. The latter part of the research helps especially in the assessment of the project from the viewpoint of one or more of the participating groups. In this paper, I shall try to interpret our latest evidence from the point of view of native northerners with unsettled land claims.

I shall therefore focus on three economic issues:

1 What are the likely cost savings from the use of a Mackenzie Valley route rather than a trans-Alaska route for the movement of natural gas from Prudhoe Bay to markets in the lower 48 states? Since the proposed pipeline passes through territory involved in native land claims, estimates of the potential value of this pipeline corridor are of obvious importance.

2 If sufficient gas is found in the Mackenzie-Beaufort region to fill half the 48-inch pipeline proposed by Canadian Arctic Gas Pipeline Ltd. (CAGPL) or all of the 42-inch pipeline proposed by Foothills Pipe Lines Ltd. what estimates can be made of the net economic benefits that would accrue, and to whom?

3 What are the economic consequences of earlier versus later development of natural gas resources in the Mackenzie Delta? There are two aspects to this question, both important. On the one hand, unless there are important economic benefits from early development, there can be no strong case made that a Mackenzie Valley pipeline should be started before settlement of native land claims. Second, if analysis shows that immediate development promises greater total benefits than later development, but will produce little direct benefits to native northerners, then deferral of development has offsetting effects whose relative size must be measured. For example, if deferral of development permits a land settlement and the design of tax, royalty, and right-of-

way terms that are significantly better than the present ones, from the point
of view of native northerners, then deferral could be to the economic advantage of northerners even if the total of potential economic rents were reduced
by deferral. By contrast, if the tax, royalty, and resource management arrangements likely to apply to immediate development are as favourable to the federal government as could reasonably be expected, and if the strength of the
native land claims were not jeopardized by development before claims settlement, then it could be in the economic interest of northerners to agree to
early development unless there were thought to be further increases likely in
the value of the northern energy resources.

Enough by way of general background. I shall proceed to report some of
our recent results, make some qualifications, and then try to sketch the implications. The results are derived from an increasingly comprehensive model of
Canadian energy supply and demand, involving estimates of demand for the
main primary energy sources in five Canadian regions, combined with models
for construction and operation of the various Mackenzie Valley pipeline proposals (as well as the El Paso and Alcan proposals for transporting Prudhoe
Bay gas by other routes) and for the supply and costs of natural gas from the
Mackenzie Delta and from non-frontier sources, conventional oil from non-
frontier sources, and synthetic oil from the Athabasca oil sands. A document
describing the most recent version of the entire energy model is available
(Helliwell *et al.* 1976). The analysis is continually being revised and extended,
as we attempt to embody the latest evidence and as we continue to improve
and refine the structure. Many individuals have been involved in the research;
the key contributors to the current pipeline research include Robert McRae,
Gerry May, Bruce Duncan, Ken Hendricks, and Don Weisbeck. The names of
the other current participants are listed in the document.

Our cost estimates for the Mackenzie Valley pipeline proposals are based
on the latest cost data submitted by CAGPL and the Foothills group to the
National Energy Board at the end of January 1976. The cost data for the
trans-Alaska and tanker route proposed by El Paso, and for the United States
portions of the Arctic Gas project are from the cost/benefit study done by
Aerospace for the US Department of the Interior. Our cost estimates for the
Alcan (Alaska highway) route for Prudhoe Bay gas are based on evidence submitted by CAGPL to the National Energy Board and by Robert Blair of
Alberta Gas Trunk Line to the House of Commons Resources Committee.
The details of the cost data and our methods of using it to construct transport
costs for natural gas are described in detail in appendix 5 of Helliwell *et al.*
(1976). Our initial assumptions about energy values are that the price of imported oil landed in Montreal will be about thirteen 1976 dollars, and that internal Canadian oil and natural gas prices will continue to rise to those levels.

Now for some results. First, what about the value of the Canadian transportation corridor for Alaskan gas? Our calculations suggest that the cost advantage of the Canadian route over the alternative trans-Alaska route proposed by El Paso has a total present value of about 3.0 billion 1976 dollars (assuming $1 Canadian = $1 U.S. in 1976). Of this amount, *none would accrue to northern natives* unless there were, say, increased pipeline right-of-way charges.

Our estimate of the net economic advantage of the Canadian route is greater than that made by the Aerospace study, primarily because their 'base case' analysis assumes that a maximum of only 1 bcfd (billion cubic feet per day) of gas will be available from the Delta, and that the United States will pay 75 per cent of the costs of the Canadian facilities, while obtaining 2.3 bcf of the systems throughput of about 3.2 bcf. By contrast, the CAGPL submission, from which our estimates are derived, assumes that shippers of Alaskan gas will pay about half of the total costs of the Canadian system and will receive a daily throughput averaging 2 bcf, half of the daily throughput.

The US share of costs might be made higher than the US share of throughput (after allowing for the greater distance travelled by the Alaskan gas) in order to share the cost advantages of the Canadian route for the Alaskan gas. However, the existing CAGPL proposal makes no allowance for any unequal sharing of costs favourable to Canadian users and there is no mechanism in place for channelling any extra payments to native northerners; further the use of more direct methods of obtaining a Canadian share in the transportation advantage (such as a throughput surcharge for Alaskan gas) has apparently been made unlikely by pending agreements between the US and Canadian federal governments. The most direct means available for native northerners to obtain a share of the transportation surplus would be through pipeline right-of-way charges. Effective negotiation of these would presumably require a prior settlement of native land claims, so that all parties should know whose rights were being transferred to whom.

To the extent that early development increases the gains for US transshippers and increases the net costs to Canadian gas users (for reasons I shall explain later), the use of a right-of-way charge that applies equally to all users is not the most effective or equitable way for native groups to use whatever land rights they have or acquire. This provides an example of policy decisions that have already been taken without apparent regard for native land claims and that operate to reduce the likely eventual value of native ownership rights.

The latest pipeline application to appear before the National Energy Board is the Alcan proposal sponsored by the Northwest Pipeline Corporation in the United States and Alberta Gas Trunk Line and Westcoast Transmission in Canada. Their idea is to transport Alaskan gas via the Trans-Alaska Pipeline

System (TAPS) oil pipeline corridor to Fairbanks, thence by a new pipeline corridor along the Alaskan highway to link up with existing pipelines at the northern edges of BC and Alberta. Thereafter, the gas would be shipped to the United States by the Westcoast Transmission (30 per cent) and Alberta Gas Trunk Line systems (AGTL) (70 per cent). This proposal provides an obvious alternative for the shipment of Alaskan gas. Using the preliminary cost estimates released by AGTL, and put through our model so as to be comparable with the other proposals, the average tariff from Prudhoe Bay to the 49th parallel (excluding transmission gas) would be about 3 cents per mcf (million cubic feet), or 5 per cent, more expensive than the Mackenzie Valley route. According to CAGPL's estimates of the costs of both routes, the Alaska highway route would be almost 25 cents per mcf more expensive.

If the Alberta Gas Trunk Line estimates turn out to be more accurate, then the Alcan route provides a cheaper alternative to the El Paso route for Alaskan gas, and hence reduces the value of, and immediate pressure for, using the Mackenzie Valley corridor as a route for Alaskan gas.

I turn now to the second question: what are the direct economic benefits and costs likely to flow from early development of Mackenzie Delta gas reserves, and to whom are they likely to accrue? Our research to date has ignored environmental costs and the direct effects on northern communities, matters which I believe to be important, and on which the Berger Inquiry has focused. For the present, we have left these matters for others to assess rather than extend our efforts into areas where we have little to contribute.

We can do slightly better when it comes to the indirect effects that development has on northern communities, for we have used the aggregate quarterly model RDX2 to indicate the macroeconomic effects of pipeline construction and operation, and it is possible to infer something about the corresponding pattern of effects in the north. For the economy as a whole, the construction of a Mackenzie pipeline induces something of a surge of activity, followed by a slump after the main construction is over. In general, the communities near the pipeline route or on the main supply lines are likely to feel these pressures in greater measure, much as has happened in Alaska in connection with the Trans-Alaska oil pipeline. To some extent it is possible to develop policies that spread the pressures and cut back on other expenditures to make room for the project. The need to develop such policies, and the difficulty in finding ones specific and flexible enough to smooth all the pressure points, help us to see the most important aspect of the issue – that in general the difficulties in providing for Canadian energy needs will be least if the lowest-cost and most easily accessible resources are developed first, but treated and conserved as more precious than their direct cost, to take account of the higher costs of later energy developments. To the extent that the cheapest sources are not developed first, and to the extent that energy is wasted by pretending that it is worth less than frontier gas will cost, our resources are misused. In terms of the economic impact of construction, over-early development of the more expensive sources needlessly creates greater national and local economic disturbances.

In general, our economic impact studies at the national level have suggested that the impacts at the national level are not beyond the powers of monetary and fiscal policies to accommodate, particularly if the planning is done with adequate care. The local economic effects are likely to raise more serious problems, but our research has not focused on them.

The more important part of the economic analysis, in my view, is that relating to the costs and benefits to the various participants. Our calculations separate the federal government and the producing firms, and show what net economic returns would accrue to each from the production of about 24 tcf (trillion cubic feet) of Mackenzie Delta gas (about 21 tcf delivered to the downstream end of the pipeline) over the life-time of a Mackenzie Valley pipeline. The well-head price of gas, against which royalties are levied, is obtained by starting with a Toronto city gate value of $2.25/mcf (in constant 1976 dollars) and subtracting the estimated TransCanada and Mackenzie Valley pipeline tariffs.

We have done the calculations separately for the Arctic Gas and Foothills proposals. In each case the net economic rents for the federal government are measured by accumulating the royalties and taxes paid and subtracting the tax revenue that the same amount of capital would generate if it were invested elsewhere in the economy. In the beginning, tax revenues are negative as capital cost allowances can be claimed against income earned elsewhere by the producing firms. The current version of the model calculates federal royalties according to the proposals announced in May 1976 (Canada, Department of Energy, Mines and Resources, 1976). We have also maintained our model of the earlier royalties and regulations, so that the two systems may be compared. Under the previous system, there was a 50 per cent royalty on the first three years of production and a 10 per cent royalty thereafter. In addition, certain lease rights were to revert to the Crown for subsequent resale. Given the slow build-up of production, we estimated that both sources of income could be approximated by a 7 per cent gross royalty for the first four years of production. Under the new system, there is a 10 per cent production royalty plus a 40 per cent progressive incremental royalty (PIR) levied only on the amount by which profits (after income taxes and production royalty) exceed

25 per cent of the depreciated value of investment. Using our current data for Delta costs and revenues, the present value of federal revenues is almost the same under the two systems, as no incremental royalty becomes payable until the fifteenth year of production.

Economic rents accruing to the producers are obtained by subtracting taxes, royalties, operating costs, depreciation, and a normal return on capital from the well-head price. The costs of exploration, development, and processing are based on the data submitted in the Foothills cost/benefit study. The rents for both parties are accumulated over the producing life of the reserves and then discounted to form a present value total measured in millions of 1976 dollars. Our calculations, for the Arctic Gas proposal using the May 1976 royalty proposals and the corporation income tax treatment established in the June 1975 federal budget, indicate net rents to the producers of about 2.1 billion 1976 dollars and to the federal government of about $2.3 billion.

What is the significance of these numbers for native land claims? The sum of the two, $4.4 billion, is the amount by which the value of 24 tcf of Delta gas exceeds its estimated costs of development and transportation. If all these estimates were certain, then this is the amount that a landlord would be able to obtain for the rights to develop that amount of Delta gas, with production starting in 1981. Thus it provides some estimate of the potential value of any land claim covering those producing properties. Some immediate cautions are in order. The current amount of proven reserves in the Delta area is 4 rather than 24 tcf, and the remainder might not be there, or might entail higher costs than estimated. Second, the cost estimates for both Mackenzie Valley pipeline proposals are likely to be on the low side. Each of the applicants wants his proposal to be less expensive than the other in order to gain NEB preference, but there is no apparent penalty to the successful applicant if the actual costs subsequently turn out to be higher than forecast.

Thus the estimate of 4.4 billion 1976 dollars for 24 tcf of Delta gas is likely to be on the high side. Even these high estimates show that Delta gas is much more costly than non-frontier gas. Our estimates for the total potential rents from non-frontier gas (if Delta gas were not developed so soon as to displace non-frontier production), assuming the NEB's latest estimate of 114 tcf ultimate non-frontier production, total about 58 billion 1976 dollars.

The rents from Delta gas transported by the Foothills system are almost exactly the same (per/mcf), because our estimates of the pipeline tariffs are almost identical, if we use both applicants' estimates of their own costs within our model framework. In terms of average tariffs expressed in 1975 cents/mcf, the Foothills system is about 7¢ per mcf more expensive north of 60°, and about 5¢ per mcf cheaper south of 60°.

Despite the uncertainty about our estimate of $4.4 billion for the rents from 24 tcf of Delta gas, the amount is substantial. The royalty rates used in our modelling are low enough that the federal government collects little more than half of the total. This has important implications for the value of native land claims, as the federal tax and royalty regulations in force at the time development is approved may well establish, at least in the eyes of the federal government and the producers, the size of the pie that is available to be shared with native groups. As for the $2.1 billion net rents not collected by the federal government, they would accrue to the shareholders of the producing firms, about 75 per cent in the United States and most of rest in southern Canada.

Now I turn, at last, to my third question. What are the likely effects of different development times for the Mackenzie Delta? First, a simple but often un-recognized point: *if* the prices of gas and oil (relative to other things) are not likely to rise further, and *if* delay would not permit significantly better planning, then deferral lowers the net economic rents available from exploiting the Delta. However, if the Delta gas is developed before it is needed (at the appropriate price) then it would be necessary to shut in non-frontier gas to make room for the Delta gas, thus lowering the net economic benefits from non-frontier gas. Only empirical analysis can show which of these effects is larger. Our calculations indicate that total Canadian benefits rise with deferral until the early 1990s, and fall thereafter. Producer rents in the Delta fall as development is deferred, while non-frontier producers and the provincial governments are better off. The federal government gains in the south and loses in the north as development is deferred, and on balance its position is almost unchanged. Deferred development lowers the US benefits from trans-shipping Alaskan gas, by postponing the savings. More importantly, substantial deferral of the Arctic Gas project would probably mean that the US would choose to send the Prudhoe Bay gas via the El Paso system (pipeline to Valdez, hence by LNG tanker to California) or by the Alcan pipeline via the Alaska highway. This would probably mean the end of the CAGPL consortium in its present form, but would not foreclose the possibilities for later shipment of Alaskan gas, if the Aerospace study for the US Department of the Interior is correct in forecasting that 45 tcf of natural gas will be discovered in Alaska by 1985.

What are the implications of all this for the potential value of native land claims? First, the native groups have at present only unsettled land claims, and the federal government has apparently not developed a taxation and royalty system that collects very efficiently the economic rents from Delta gas, and has apparently decided not to make any attempt to share in the cost savings arising from the shipment of Alaskan gas through Canada. If deferral would permit native groups to achieve a more effective land settlement, or to use to greater effect whatever landlord rights they do acquire, then deferral is likely to improve the value of their share of economic benefits from a pipeline.

Even if it were not true that deferral promised net economic advantages to native groups, the Indian Brotherhood of the NWT and other native groups have announced a clear preference, on environmental and social grounds, for later rather than earlier development. However, it is very likely that economic factors also favour deferral from the point of view of native people, because they regard pipeline approval before a full land settlement as likely to jeopardize the nature and terms of the settlement.

What about southern economic interests? I have argued that from the point of view of non-frontier producers and Canadian consumers, there are likely to be net economic advantages from deferral for ten or more years. The only net losers from deferral are likely to be the Mackenzie Delta producers. If deferral were to permit less costly routes or techniques to be developed, or if there were continued increases in oil and gas prices in the next twenty years, then even the producers would be better off. And, on the other side, sharp drops in energy prices or discovery of cheaper sources elsewhere might render the Delta deposits uneconomic for either immediate or deferred development. Deferral would also permit further exploration to show whether there is enough gas in the Delta to support a transportation system and to insure against the awful possibility of rushing through a pipeline to the wrong place.

Finally, I should point out the tight but often ignored link between the question of economic rents and the question of southern need for Arctic gas. On the one hand, it is often argued by oil industry spokesmen that the costs of finding, developing, and transporting Arctic gas are so high that there is little scope for landlords, be they native or white, to charge a substantial price, by royalty or whatever, for access to the resource. On the other hand, it is argued that southern Canada urgently needs Arctic gas, meaning that there are no alternatives available at anything like comparable cost. These two arguments are contradictory. If the Arctic gas is much preferred over any alternative form of domestic or imported energy, then it has a high resource value on which the landlord has a primary claim. If, on the other hand, the Arctic gas and its transportation system are so costly that there is little scope for collecting taxes or royalties, then no importance can be attached to claims of urgency. After all, if Arctic gas is as expensive as available substitutes, then there is no economic need for it. It matters little if the substitute is imported, as the price of foreign exchange will simply take the level required to encourage exports (and discourage other imports) so as to re-establish the foreign balance of payments.

It should be quite clear, by now, that it cannot be true that Arctic gas is urgently required *and* that there is little surplus resource value on which to base native land claims. Our research indicates that *neither* position is well established by the evidence submitted by Foothills and CAGPL. If enough gas is eventually found to justify a pipeline, then there is likely to be a substantial resource value unless the costs of development and transportation are substantially higher than forecast in the Foothills and CAGPL submissions. On the other hand, the total national economic advantage would be better served by using lower-cost sources first, and thus deferring development of Arctic gas.

REFERENCES

Canada, Department of Energy, Mines and Resources (1976), *Statement of Policy: Proposed Petroleum and Natural Gas Act and Gas Land Regulations* (Ottawa)
Helliwell, John F., *et al.* (1976), *An Integrated Model for Energy Policy Analysis* (Vancouver: UBC Programme in Natural Resource Economics)
United States, Department of the Interior (1975), *Alaskan Natural Gas Transportation Systems: Economic and Risk Analysis* (Washington)

From Underdevelopment to Development

Mel Watkins

The pipeline applicants, Arctic Gas and Foothills, assert in effect that the proposed gas pipeline provides a new opportunity for northern native people. The form that opportunity is said to take is the increased potential for wage-employment. They point to the extent of present unemployment among native people as evidence of the need for this opportunity, though they presumably overestimate this to the same extent as they underestimate the number of active hunters, fishers, and trappers. In any event, they have some difficulty squaring their assertion with the extent of earlier job-creating projects, notably in mining, but resolve the matter by insisting that the pipeline will constitute a break with the past. They emphasize that the jobs created in the operations phase, but not of course in the construction phase, will be permanent rather than transitory – though, again, they beg the question of how this is different from mining, as well as the question of how permanent is permanent. Finally, they appeal to the training program for northerners. They are right to do this, since it would appear to be the only novel feature of the pipeline relative to the other earlier projects, though it is certainly a moot point whether such a modest program can reasonably bear the weight of legitimizing the pipeline as a break with the past.

As well, the applicants assert their respect for native land claims, and urge both the native organizations and the government to settle them so that their projects can proceed. They appear to assert that a pipeline prior to a land settlement will not prejudice the claim, though they simultaneously pretend not to know what the claim is really about in the absence of specific details. They refuse to accept the Dene position that a pipeline can under no circumstances be started prior to a land settlement. They do not appear to have responded to the assertion that the Dene land claim is centrally about the political, and human, right to alternative development.

If we are to evaluate these assertions, and consider the probable impact of a pipeline, we need to know something about, first, the nature of past development and the present condition of native people, and second, the nature and extent of the land claim, or the nature of alternative development, both for their own sake and for the purpose of assessing prejudice to the claim.

At the same time, we can speak to the positive assertions of the Dene: that they own 450,000 square miles of land; that their title to the land should be recognized rather than extinguished; that their aboriginal and human rights transcend property rights to include political rights, namely, the right to self-determination as a nation; that their desire for economic independence can be met by creating alternative community-based economic development under their control; that further development, and particularly the proposed pipeline, threatens gravely to prejudice the land claim by eroding their aboriginal and human rights.

Past and present development

The first notion of which we should disabuse ourselves is that what the applicants have in mind for the North is novel from any historical perspective. Quite the contrary. The history of Canada, as written by the greatest of our historians, is as a succession of staple exports from successive geographic frontiers to serve the needs of more advanced industrial areas. The great export commodities have been fish, fur, square timber, lumber, wheat, pulp and paper, minerals, and oil and gas. The consequences for Canada have been profound:

Energy has been directed toward the exploitation of staple products and the tendency has been cumulative ... Energy in the colony was drawn into the production of the staple commodity both directly and indirectly. Population was involved directly in the production of the staple and indirectly in the production of facilities promoting production. Agriculture, industry, transportation, trade, finance, and governmental activities tend to become subordinate to the production of the staple for a more highly specialized manufacturing community. (Innis, 1930)

And again:

Concentration on the production of staples for export to more highly industrialized areas in Europe and later in the United States had broad implications for the Canadian economic, political and social structure. Each staple in its turn left its stamp, and the shift to new staples invariably produced periods of crises in which adjustments in the old structure were painfully made and a new pattern created in relation to a new staple. (Innis, 1948)

The methodology of this 'staples approach' is directly helpful to us in considering the matter of 'impact.' The impact of the proposed pipeline is simply the 'stamp' of the oil and gas industry on Canada in general and the North in particular. The North is experiencing 'the shift to a new staple'; the result is a 'period of crisis' and of 'painful adjustments.'

What is the impact of a staple? First, all of the staple trades have in common a bias towards serving the needs of more advanced metropolitan areas – once France, then Britain, and now the United States. This is clearly relevant when we are told, as in the present case, that the Dene interest must yield to the higher national interest. Not only is the hinterland interest being made subservient to the national interest, but by some sleight of hand the national interest is equated with the metropolitan interest.

Second, each staple leaves its particular stamp. Two great staple trades have dominated the North, the fur trade and now, increasingly, minerals (mining and petroleum, the economic characteristics of which are the same, that is, the highly capital-intensive exploitation of non-renewable resources). These two staples have had profoundly different economic impacts on native people.

But first we need to retreat for a moment and see how the aboriginal people fit, in the most fundamental sense, into this approach to the story of Canadian development, past and present. Innis makes the essential point, at least implicitly, when he writes 'Fundamentally the civilization of North America is the civilization of Europe,' and again 'Canada has remained fundamentally a product of Europe' (Innis, 1930). The Indian way of life, indeed the Indian himself, has been swept aside. Only in the era of the fur trade was the Indian functional to the Euro-Canadian, and everywhere the fur trade retreated in the face of settlement and was ultimately obliterated by it. The fate of the Indian was simply to become irrelevant. It is that fate, which was visited upon the Indian as the whiteman's frontier moved inexorably west and north, that now faces the Dene. Today native people are the majority in the NWT but, of course, that has always been true initially in each of the successive frontiers.

The most dramatic demonstration of this functional irrelevance of the Indian is to be found in the very terminology that historians use to characterize Canada – and other like cases, such as the United States, Australia and New Zealand. Their aboriginal populations notwithstanding, they are called 'empty lands' or 'areas of recent settlement' or 'new countries' or 'undeveloped areas' or simply 'the frontier.' Their histories can be written, and are written, as the story of successive waves of white settlers exploiting new frontiers and transplanting European institutions. The resistance of the Indian – for there has been resistance at every step – becomes in the history books little more than a lengthy footnote to the main story. The Riel uprising is crushed, Riel is hanged, and he casts his long shadow over subsequent history not because he was a native resistance leader but because he was a Catholic.

There is, then, an awful truth about the manner in which this country was 'born,' and has since been successively rejuvenated. We cannot change that history, but we can learn from it and resolve 'never again.' Put differently, the exigencies of staple production must make allowance in the North, for the first time, for the reality of native rights; unless that is done, nothing will really change.

Let us now look briefly at the specific and differing impacts of fur and minerals as staples. To begin, there is the theoretical question of the mechanisms by which production and trade of a particular staple leaves its stamp. It is clear from the quotations from Innis that these are pervasive, but at least with respect to the central economic mechanisms they can be broken down by focusing on the actual mode of staple production and the linkages to other sectors of the economy.

The mode of production can be understood for present purposes as the particular mix of factors of production - of land (that is, natural resources), labour, and capital - used to produce the staple within, at any moment of time, a given technological and institutional framework. The linkages are the spread effects from the staple sector to other sectors of the economy, and particularly the local economy, through the market mechanism. They can be conveniently classified as three-fold: forward linkage, that is, further processing of the staple; backward linkage, that is, the production of inputs including capital goods for use in production of the staple; and final demand linkage, that is, the spending of the income received by the commodity producers or workers on consumer goods. In each case, the stronger the linkages, the greater the income generated in the local economy - or, in the language of the economist, the higher the multiplier.

The prosecution of the fur trade depended, at least initially in each region into which the trade expanded, on the Indian as fur-gatherer. As such the Indian was a commodity producer, not a wage-earner, and the fur trade was literally a trade, or a commercial activity, not an industrial activity. The Indian became dependent to the extent that he became vulnerable to the exigencies of the trade, but he did not have to make two critical and traumatic adjustments that result from imposed industrialization. Firstly, he did not have to become a wage-earner, and secondly, which is really the opposite side of the coin, he did not have to yield up his ownership of the land. To put the matter differently, neither his labour-time nor his land had to become themselves marketable commodities.

This point is of the first importance. For the student of economic history in general, no theme is so compelling as the process by which land-bound people - typically agrarian but sometimes nomadic - are turned, against their will, into industrial workers. In general, it has not been a voluntary process, the mere offering of another option as the applicants like to phrase it. Rather, the tendency has been for people to be pushed off the land or to have others sell it from beneath their feet. To turn land-bound people into landless wage-earners has typically involved coercion.

Now mineral production (including petroleum) is an industry not a trade, and it needs both rights to the use of land and people who will work for a wage. The Hudson's Bay Company, as a fur-trading company, did not need to own the land; indeed, it was in its interest to let the Indians own the land, the better to trap on it, and to discourage white settlement. Only when settlement overrode the fur trade, or promised imminently to do so, as it did in the West, did the Bay see fit to transform itself into a real-estate company and to pretend, successfully as it turned out, that *it* owned Indian land and was entitled to compensation rather than the Indians.

But for the mining and petroleum companies, no such ambiguity is tolerable. Ownership arrangements with respect to the land must be such that they have a clear right to take minerals from under the land and transport minerals over the land. Hence, in the context of the present situation, they act on the assumption that the land is not Dene land, but Crown land, and if that is not so now it should be made so by a land settlement that extinguishes aboriginal title; the land, then, either is or must become Crown land, and the companies know full well the propensity of the Crown to let them extract resources. Furthermore, since 'land' is simply a commodity, should the Dene perchance own some land that is needed - either because title has not been resolved or because property rights have been vested with the Dene as part of a land settlement - the companies reply that they can buy it, and should the Dene be unwilling to sell, the companies say that they can, with the help of the Crown, expropriate it.

This helps us to understand what a 'land settlement' must necessarily mean to the industry, namely, extinguishing native title to the land or, as a minimum, limiting any recognition of aboriginal rights to property rights subject to expropriation, so as to remove an impediment to industrial activity.

The industry needs labour as well, but here we do not need to be cynical to see that Dene labour is hardly so essential as Dene land. Non-native labour is generally readily available from the South - and this is particularly so now given the extent of unemployment - and has the advantage that it is not 'raw' labour but trained and disciplined labour. The record of the mining industry, or of the Imperial Oil refinery at Norman Wells, in this regard, namely, their failure over long periods of time to employ much native labour and, when they did, mostly in the most menial and casual occupations, is sufficient demonstration of how the economics of the matter works. True, the government now insists on the employment of native labour, and industry is generally compliant - in part because much of the training costs are paid by the government - but the motives involved are at best mixed. It is good public relations for both government and industry, and in general has more to do with politics than with economics. And there are incidental advantages. To the extent it works, it means less native use of the land, relative to what would otherwise be the case, and hence can be alleged to diminish the potency of a land claim based on land use (though not, of course, the possessory rights that flow from land occupancy since time immemorial). For the government, the whole scheme can to some extent be seen as a substitute for welfare. When all is said and done, what is involved for the Indian is a swap - a job in the wage economy for abandoning and yielding up the land. We need to have only the slightest knowledge of the value of the natural resources of the North to the companies to know what an unequal bargain that is for the Dene.

We can get some idea of that value by enquiring about the role of capital and the nature of its return, and a closely related matter, namely, who gets the return to 'land,' or 'economic rent.' Up to a point, the matter is straightforward. Under the market system, the providers of capital receive dividends and interest. All we need add is that the owners of this capital may reside outside the region - as they clearly do in the cases of both the fur trade and mineral production in the North - and in that case no benefit therefrom accrues to the residents of the region.

But what if staple production yields profits above and beyond those necessary to service capital? This is not a hypothetical matter, but is rather to be expected in the nature of the case. The main reason is that staple production necessarily means exploitation of natural resources, or of 'land,' and since the latter is scarce, it is likely to command its own reward. The critical question then becomes who gets the reward, or who appropriates the rents. Logic suggests that the answer is the owner of the land. If, as is alleged in the North, the Crown owns the land, then it should get the rents, and that is a rationale for royalties and other forms of taxation of the resource industries. If the Crown fails to appropriate the rents - as it largely does in the North and as it apparently intends to continue doing in the future - they are transformed into 'super-profits' and are appropriated by the owners of the capital or, in effect, the corporation itself for purposes of re-investment. There is, however, no reason to expect that they will be re-invested within the staple-producing region which generated them, and every reason to expect that they will not be re-invested in the region in other activities that serve local priorities. What tends to happen, then, is that the return to capital and to land leaves the region; all that remains is the return to labour, and that only to the extent it is resident labour.

To cast the Dene simply as wage-earners, as the applicants do, is then not only to cast them in a role they may not want, but to deny them their role as the land-owners who should be entitled to appropriate the rents from projects which they choose to let proceed on their land. That denial is critical, for it means that the once-and-for-all rents generated within the region, from non-renewable resources that are in due course depleted, are ultimately re-invested at the behest of the corporation outside the region, rather than being re-invested within the region, by the people themselves, in activities based on renewable resources that could survive after the non-renewable resources are exhausted.

In this respect, the oil industry is no different from the fur trade. The Hudson's Bay Company appropriated such enormous surpluses from the fur trade that it is now a major retailer, real estate developer, and shareholder in the oil and gas industry. Indeed, beyond that, the fortunes that originated in the fur trade went on to spawn yet greater fortunes in banking and railways. Of what benefit has this been to the northern natives who produced the fur?

When the resource is non-renewable, as it is for mining and oil and gas, the major legacy of failing to keep the surpluses in the region to seed other activities is the well-known Canadian phenomenon of the ghost town. As Northrop Frye observed in his 1976 'Images of Canada' television special on the CBC, 'Canada is full of ghost towns: visible ruins unparalleled in Europe.' The ghost town symbolizes everything that the native people, as *the* long-term residents of the North, have to fear from the present mode of staple production; for by then who knows what cumulative damage will have been done to their land and its ability to support them?

There is also the matter of linkages of the staple sector to other sectors of the local economy. None of these linkages operate so as to create much economic activity in the North beyond the primary sector itself, and there is little reason to expect this to change. The primary product tends to be exported in a relatively unprocessed form, and there is a high propensity to import both capital goods and consumer goods. Rather, the linkages tend to generate economic activity in southern Canada, the US, and elsewhere, thereby creating benefits outside the North. (This does *not* mean that there is necessarily a net benefit to southern Canadians. Whether or not there is depends as well on the effects of frontier development on primary product prices, and hence indirectly on the prices of other commodities embodying the primary product. If the price of the staple rises to make frontier production possible, this will lower the real incomes of those who, directly or indirectly, consume the staple. This phenomenon is clearly relevant with respect to high-cost northern oil and gas and very probably makes the net benefit to the great majority of southern Canadians negative.)

Predictably, the tactic of the businessmen and government of the staple-exporting region is to attempt to increase the linkages within the region. Whatever crumbs they achieve by this strategy are, of course, necessarily obtained by their having to opt wholeheartedly for continuing staple production. Hence, it is no surprise that local business interests in the North are solidly behind the pipeline, and that the territorial government conceives of Indian economic development as helping the Dene to get a piece of the action that will be generated in other sectors by the pipeline – in spite of the fact that the latter has about it something of the aura of asking the condemned man to take up rope manufacturing.

Nor can it be assumed that an existing local enterprise will necessarily reap any benefit at all from a resource boom; it may even be left worse off. In his testimony before the Berger Inquiry at the community hearing in Fort Resolution, Father Lou Menez gave no less than four examples for that community alone – in the fur business, river transportation, sawmilling, and commercial fishing – where existing native involvement was pushed aside by subsequent rounds of activity. Some of those awaiting the pipeline will experience not a linkage effect but a shrinkage effect.

It was noted at the beginning of this analytical discourse that staple production takes place within a framework of technology and institutions. These are not ordained from on high, but are man-made; nevertheless, for the staple-producing region they are largely imposed, being created and controlled by outside interests. This is very clear today in the mineral sector of the North, where the technology is highly capital-intensive and a small number of large companies are dominant. In so far as the technology is difficult to alter, the message for local people, and above all for the Dene as the permanent residents, is, again, not to be satisfied with merely being wage-earners in the mineral sector, but rather to focus on the rents which otherwise accrue to capital and are drained away. In so far as the corporations, as the dominant institutions, are difficult to alter, and the government is an alien institution subservient to corporate needs, the relevant message for the Dene is to create a new institutional framework within the North under the control of the Dene to which these entities must adapt.

Large-scale resource projects are said by their proponents to create 'development.' In fact, for native people what has resulted is properly characterized as 'underdevelopment.' The process of underdevelopment permits of a reasonably precise definition, namely, the 'blockage of potential, sustained economic and social development geared to local human needs (Rothney and Watson, 1975). The primary mechanism by which local development is suppressed is by the outward drain of economic surplus from the region. The most significant loss from the failure to retain surplus is the destruction of local self-determination.

Let no one doubt that the outflow of income generated in the North is large. This is evident from an examination of the social accounts of the North which has been done by John Palmer of Indian and Northern Affairs for the period 1967 to 1970. In 1970, gross national product per capita for all of Canada was $3,866, while gross domestic product per capita (conceptually virtually the same as Canadian GNP) for the NWT was much higher at $5,311. Now the high figure for the North is because GDP includes all income originating in the North, and hence includes non-resident earnings of both individuals and corporations, but that only demonstrates the extent to which wealth is in fact created in the North but drained out as wages and salaries to southerners and cash flow from northern businesses to southern interests. In 1970, of GDP for *both* the Yukon and Northwest Territories of $266.1 million, $80.4 million was not retained in the North, $32.2 million going out as wages and salaries and $48.2 million as business cash flow.

Other comparisons are possible for the single year 1969. Per capita personal income (the income actually received by persons) was $2,915 for all Canadians, approximately $1,100 for Treaty Indians and Inuit of the NWT, and approximately $3,000 for other residents of the NWT. Total native personal income (with native defined, by those who collected the data, as Treaty Indians and Inuit) is estimated as $20.5 million in 1969 – though this is clearly too low because of an underestimate of the value of country food. In that same year, the gross return on capital (before tax) in the mining sector in the NWT was $37.4 million, of which only $4.6 million was retained in the North. Arvin Jelliss' rent estimates for the producing mines of the NWT show economic rents proper – after allowing for a 15 per cent return on capital, net of taxes and royalties – of $15.9 million in 1970 (and very much higher in 1973 and 1974).

The ultimate hallmark of underdevelopment is marginality. Economically, it manifests itself as poverty, unemployment, and welfare. (Rather than seeing welfare as 'charity,' we should appreciate its hidden dimensions. For the Dene, it avoids integration into the wage economy, and is therefore a form of resistance. For the dominant society, it is something it can afford, for there are not that many Dene, and the long-run effect of welfare, to the extent it demoralizes and degrades people, discourages concerted use of the land, and thus helps to dispossess the Dene of their land.) Socially, it manifests itself in alcoholism, family breakdown, and suicide. Politically, it manifests itself in feelings of hopelessness and apathy.

The Dene have so far been spared the fulness of that fate; they are, as the applicants like to say, in a state of transition. But the direction of history is clear. It has recently been succinctly summarized by the anthropologist, Peter Douglas Elias:

Indian socio-economic phenomena must be studied within the historic and
contemporary framework of the development of industrial, class-capitalist
Canada. With the passage of time, Canada tended to acquire the 'typical'
characteristics of class-capitalist society. The producers, in this case the
Native people of Canada, were separated from the means of production,
embodied, essentially, in the land and the products of the land. The means
of production became concentrated and monopolized in the hands of a single
social class, and natives became a class owning no possessions and, ultimately,
having no exchangeable commodity other than labour. Even this 'typical'
model of capitalist development was surpassed by natives becoming a permanently underemployed class subsisting on social assistance ... An examination
of the history of native and white contact reveals the processes that culminated in the total integration of Native peoples into contemporary Canadian
society as permanent members of the underclass.

Hugh Brody tells us that the process is at work today with respect to the
native people of the Eastern Arctic:

The most recent trends are pushing native people increasingly towards the
lowest and least certain rung on the national class ladder: if separated from
his own means of production and unable to have a sure relationship to the
intruders' means of production, the Eskimo – like many Canadian and American Indians before him – will be turned into a migrant worker, a casual la-
bourer, and – as this lumpenproletarian condition develops – prostitute, petty
thief and beggar. Abundant signs of this course of events are already visible.

It must be insisted upon that the purpose of northern native land claims is
neither more nor less than to subvert this terrible historic process.

It is important to understand as well that this way of analysing the condition of native people is very different from those who insist, explicitly or implicitly, that the reality we are observing, particularly in the North, is a 'dual
economy.' According to this view, the North is a two-sector economy, con-
sisting of a 'modern' sector and a 'traditional' sector, and these two sectors
are substantially separate. The 'modern' sector is seen as essentially an 'en-
clave,' where 'development' takes place, while the 'traditional' sector is stag-
nant and full of problems, and is not experiencing the benefits of 'development.' The logic of this position is that the solution lies in moving people out
of the 'traditional' sector and into the 'modern' sector. The transition, though
painful, is necessary. At the end of the road – or in this case, at the end of the
pipeline – what will be created is a one-sector 'modern' economy with everybody experiencing the benefits of 'development.'

The thrust of my argument is very different. The concept of dual economy
is not helpful in analysing the history of the Mackenzie District either in the
era of the fur trade or in the recent, and present, era of mineral production.
In the past, when the fur trade was dominant, the economy was a one-sector
native economy with trapping commercialized. The Dene benefited, though

at the long-run cost of dependency. The moral seems clear: had the Dene controlled the fur trade, rather than the Bay Company, tendencies to 'mining' and
consequent depletion could have been curtailed; surpluses could have been kept
in the region to permit more diversified development around renewable resources, rather than being used to build edifices in Winnipeg and Toronto; and
white trappers – who became an increasingly serious problem for the Dene in
this century, as Father Fumoleau has shown – could have been excluded, assuming the political rights of the native majority were allowed to express themselves.

Today, the economy is a two-sector economy with the mineral sector
added to the pre-existing one-sector economy. But the two sectors are anything but separate. Rather, the operation of the 'new' sector works, through a
variety of mechanisms, to underdevelop the 'old' sector. The economic surplus generated by the 'new' sector is either used to generate further activity in
the 'new' sector or is drained out of the region; none even 'trickles down' to
the 'old' sector. The white settlers attracted by the 'new' sector impose alien
institutions and pre-empt the power of the native people; the native people
experience degradation and anomie.

Again, there would seem to be a clear moral: *if* non-renewable resource
exploitation is to continue, then instead of integrating the Dene into a one-
sector economy – which they say they do not want and which does not
appear to have worked elsewhere in Canada – what should be considered is
creating a two-sector economy which has the real promise of being beneficial
to the Dene. That is, instead of blithely assuming that a dual economy exists
today but should be encouraged to wither away in the long run, we should
see that what could be created is a two-sector economy where the two sectors
would co-exist harmoniously. That would require us to look carefully at the
means by which the present mechanisms of underdevelopment could be
turned into mechanisms of development.

The conclusion to this point is that staple production, by its inherent
nature, brings into play powerful structural and determinative factors. The
inference is that these structural tendencies can be broken only by new institutional arrangements that permit of genuine development.

The land claim and alternative development

The problem that some people may have in understanding the nature and extent of the land claim, is that both the word 'land' and the word 'claim' are
somewhat misleading. To use the word 'claim' is to imply that native people
are claiming their homeland and rights; while the erosions of colonialism are
real, we should at least say *reclaim*. But perhaps the best word is 'declaration'
(as in Dene Declaration), that is, the Dene are declaring their rights; my dic-

tionary gives as the meaning of declare 'make known, proclaim publicly'; that is, it is something the declarant already knows.

To the Euro-Canadian, the word 'land' conjures up *property rights*, and property means something that is marketable and subject to expropriation. Clearly the word 'land' means much more than that to the Dene and, specifically, in Euro-Canadian language, includes rights of control or *political rights*. The collective expression of political rights is what we would customarily call 'self-determination.' By 'land claim,' then, the Dene mean 'a declaration of the right to self-determination'; thus the Dene Declaration *is* the central statement of their claim.

Now, self-determination is a many-faceted phenomenon, with different dimensions reinforcing each other. Thus, significant economic independence, while it cannot in itself be sufficient, is nevertheless necessary for self-determination. Indeed, in so far as the Dene cannot achieve political independence – for they accept that they are part of Canada – the degree of economic independence needed may become that much more important.

What is here called 'economic independence' is what the Dene call 'alternative development.' That term can be understood to mean an 'alternative' to the 'development' of the non-renewable resource sector, which, in fact, creates underdevelopment for native people. Along the lines suggested earlier, it could be seen as meaning a two-sector economy, that is, a non-renewable resource sector under white ownership but subject to Dene control, and a renewable resource sector under Dene ownership and control.

Take the renewable resource sector first. A strong, indeed compelling case can surely be made for exclusive Dene rights in this sector, not only to hunt, fish, and trap but with respect to the whole area of game management – indeed, of all renewable resource management including forests and water. While non-Dene northern residents and the bureaucracy of the territorial government might be expected to resist this logic, it could be acceptable to the developers and the federal government, for whom the main chance is non-renewable resources (with the single exception of hydro power). But there are hidden implications not only for the developers – as we shall see directly – but also for the Dene.

For the Dene, what is at issue is not only the *protection* of their traditional economy but the right, indeed the necessity, to *create* their own contemporary economy around renewable resources. Just as it is increasingly recognized that the genuine development of the Third World hinges on agrarian reform, on the modernization of agriculture to serve domestic needs, so the genuine development of the North hinges on the modernization of the renewable resources sector by the Dene to serve Dene needs. Productivity must be improved and, given the extent both of present underemployment and the rapid growth of the native population, the sector must be expanded so that more people can be gainfully engaged in it. It would appear that the Dene prefer involvement in the renewable resource sector to involvement, at least on a full-time basis, in the non-renewable resource sector, but a restructuring of the renewable resource sector must take place so that it becomes a clearly viable sector in material terms. Given the government's obsession with the non-renewable resource sector to the virtual exclusion of all other considerations, such restructuring is, to say the least, unlikely to take place except in the context of a land settlement and its subsequent implementation. In any event, it will hardly constitute Dene development unless it is done by the Dene themselves.

It would be a considerable advance to have the recognition of exclusive Dene rights to harvest and to manage renewable resources, but it would not be sufficient. There are two reasons why this is so, that is, there are at least two identifiable mechanisms of underdevelopment which impinge on the renewable resource sector from the non-renewable resource sector and which would have to be converted into mechanisms of development.

The first is that activity in the non-renewable resource sector does damage to the renewable resource base and thereby threatens the continuing viability of that sector. The Dene can only be effectively protected against this by having themselves the power to protect their land. Even the exclusive right to use the renewable resources will be of insufficient avail if the right is not protected. Hence, alternative development *must* include the right to control over the non-renewable resource sector so as to limit environmental degradation and competing uses to an extent that is tolerable to the Dene.

The second mechanism of underdevelopment is the failure of economic surplus generated in the non-renewable resource sector to accrue to the benefit of the renewable resource sector. What is at issue here is not only the right of the land-owner to appropriate the rent, but the loss of the potential to create Dene development when that does not happen. Put more concretely, to create a viable Dene renewable resource sector requires both capital goods and Dene with both 'traditional' and 'modern' skills. Both of these, in turn, require money. So long as the money is made available under the white man's control – whether it be so-called Indian economic development funds under government auspices, or whether it be the building and operating of schools that destroy all-round Dene skills – then Dene development is a contradiction in terms. Hence, the right to alternative development must include the right to tax the non-renewable resource sector, or impose royalties thereon, so as to fund the Dene economy, and the Dene institutions, which will permit of continuing Dene development.

This is not to pretend to make a judgment about exactly how much rent should go to the Dene, but some principles can be laid down. First, given the observed failure of the government to come anywhere near to appropriating fully economic rents in the North and the apparent intention to continue to operate that way for the indefinite future, there is a good deal of room for the Dene to appropriate rents at no cost to the great majority of southern Canadians, who are not shareholders in the oil and mining industries, but solely at the cost of reducing the super-profits of the corporations. Secondly, the Dene would have the right to forgo rent by vetoing projects, or short of that, compelling changes in them that would increase costs to the companies and hence lessen the rents available for appropriation. A specific variant on this - which has received the tentative blessing of the Science Council - would be to discourage new town sites, particularly for mines, and generally encourage the flying in and out of personnel from the south; this would presumably increase the costs to the companies, but would not necessarily increase the true social costs which include large costs for infrastructure, mostly borne not by the companies but rather by governments and individuals. Thirdly, if rents accruing to the Dene are to be justified by some criteria based on need - that is, the Dene should get enough but not too much - then the criteria implicit in this analysis are simply what is necessary both to provide capital for community-based economic development - until it becomes viable and self-sustaining and has created full employment in the communities - and to permit the on-going subsidization of Dene institutions; if schools are included in the latter because the Dene were to so wish, then it should be borne in mind that there is no necessary net cost to society since the schools are now funded by the government rather than by the Dene themselves. A final observation on this third principle is to remind ourselves that the Indian people have a tradition of sharing; in spite of statements sometimes made to the contrary, there is no evidence the Dene are asking for a 'king's ransom.'

A major theme of this paper is that a concern with *economic* development compels us to concern ourselves with *political* control. In institutional terms this implies, in the context of a land settlement, both the right of the Dene to create their own institutions and the need to limit full political rights to long-term residents of the North; specifically, the logic of this argument, though focused on the economic, strongly supports a residency rule for participation in local and territorial elections, such as the ten-year residency rule proposed by the native organizations.

Conclusion

The most persistent argument used by developers, private and public, is that large-scale resource projects serve the 'public interest.' If the residents of the region where the project is to take place object, in the final analysis they are put down by appeal to the 'public interest.' This is justified by saying that the 'national interest' must override the 'regional interest,' with the reality for contemporary large-scale energy resource projects being that the relevant 'regional interest' is the 'native interest.' The native interest – which is real – is then disposed of either by saying, in effect, that it must, regrettably, be overridden, or by asserting that in some long-run sense the two interests are really identical. Yet, virtually without exception, the massive energy projects underway or planned for Northern Canada serve outside needs – and by that I mean needs external to Canada. So the choice is not, in fact, simply between the national interest and the regional native interest. Typically, in this century, there is the overriding American, or continental, interest, and it cannot be simply assumed that what serves the American interest automatically serves the national interest. In terms of the applicants, Arctic Gas clearly serves, first and foremost, the American interest, since it wishes to transport natural gas from one part of the United States to another part of the United States – a kind of contemporary version of the Panama Canal. Foothills, properly viewed, serves the continental interest, since an alternative to its pipeline for some time at least – and which could have been done some time ago – is to eliminate exports of gas to the US; furthermore, were it to get the government nod then, like Arctic Gas, it would have to go to bed with the same US-controlled producing companies. Also, the Arctic Gas proposal, and now Foothill's Fairbanks corridor proposal, appear to hinge on a treaty with the US guaranteeing safe passage of American gas through Canada; the erosion of Canadian sovereignty implicit in such a treaty is reminiscent of the by-gone era of the DEW-line in the North.

A significant dimension of the choice, then is choosing between the interests of non-Canadians and the interests of native people who are Canadians; it is of the essence of the nature of the nation-state that it should be biased in favour of its own citizenry.

It is not only the North, as the 'new frontier,' which is driven by the imperatives of staple production. So too, after close to four centuries, is Canada as a whole. We cannot forever grow by expanding into new geographic frontiers, for we are running out of places to go – and there is little merit in emulating the example of the US after its frontier closed around 1890, which finally landed it in Vietnam. The time may not be too far distant when some considerable restructuring of the Canadian economy, away from its staple-export-bias to meeting the needs of Canadians to a greater extent within itself, will be necessary. In any event, it is long overdue, and the need for a humane approach to further northern development is the best possible reason for beginning the task of restructuring now.

Many native people in this country are in their present impoverished position because of what has been done to them in the past. We can specify the mechanisms of underdevelopment by which the damage has been done. We can work out the means by which these mechanisms can be transformed into mechanisms of development. What excuse can there be for not doing it?

The Indian people, right across Canada, self-evidently need Indian economic development under Indian control. That does not mean a stark choice between either 'traditional' activity or wage-employment with non-Indian controlled enterprises. There *is* a third way, the way of alternative development.

The Dene assert that starting a pipeline prior to a land settlement would gravely prejudice that possibility. It is difficult to see how it could be otherwise. The companies ask: how can we avoid prejudice? The answer, which is understandably rejected by them, is that their very presence in the North before the Dene have reclaimed their historic rights, constitutes prejudice. They did not come with the consent of the Dene, so they should not be there. If they wish to be there, and to stay there, they must try to strike a bargain with the Dene. The role of the government is to let this happen, to give the Dene the space they need – the geographic space and the political space – knowing that what redounds to the benefit of its least prosperous citizens must ultimately redound to the prosperity of the democratic state.

REFERENCES

Brody, Hugh, *The People's Land: Eskimos and Whites in the Eastern Arctic* (London 1975)
Elias, Peter Douglas, *Metropolis and Hinterland in Northern Manitoba* (Winnipeg 1975)
Fumoleau, Rene, OMI, *As Long as This Land Shall Last, A History of Treaty 8 and Treaty 11, 1870-1939* (Toronto 1975)
Innis, H.A., *The Fur Trade in Canada: An Introduction to Canadian Economic History* (1930; 2nd ed., Toronto 1956)
- *Empire and Communications* (London 1948)
Palmer, John, *Measurement of the Value of Economic Activity in the North*, Department of Indian Affairs and Northern Development (Ottawa 1974)
Rothney, Russ, and Steve Watson, 'A Brief Economic History of Northern Manitoba' (mimeo 1975)
Science Council of Canada, *Discussion Paper on Northern Development* (Ottawa 1975)

Rights

The Colonial Experience

Peter Puxley

Over the past few years, I have sought to understand the nature of a society which, in spite of its obvious affluence, continues to exploit and ride roughshod over so many of its members, all the while appealing to some mythical 'public interest.' Since this public interest clearly does not include my interest or those of significant sectors of this society, it seems to me to be a term well worth demystifying. It has been my experience that the Dene struggle for recognition helps to clarify the nature of the larger reality all Canadians inhabit and can contribute to a more authentic definition of public interest.

I accept as given that any real change in the situation of the Dene, and by this I mean change which results in a real degree of political independence on their part, will demand an accommodation on the other side of the *relationship*, that is, from those forces now exercising almost unlimited authority over Dene life. However, to effect a significant change in this relationship will involve, first of all, understanding it in all its ramifications, both structural and psychological. This is the task ahead for the Dene and one in which any Canadian has an interest.

If it can be shown that the product of a colonial relationship is dehumanization, then we must assume that the relationship is opposed to the development of not only the colonized but also the colonizer. If human life entails acting out a uniquely human vocation, then the colonial relationship destroys rather than creates life. In this regard, the assumption that so-called 'social impact' relates only to the experience of those who are unfortunate enough to be on the receiving end of colonial projects is quite incorrect. The social impact can also be determined in the lives of those who serve this dehumanizing process.

To quote Paulo Freire:

Every relationship of domination, of exploitation, of oppression, is by definition violent, whether or not the violence is expressed by drastic means. In such a relationship, dominator and dominated alike are reduced to things – the former dehumanized by an excess of power the latter by lack of it. And things cannot love.

The ability of men to develop themselves is dependent in part on their grasp of reality, while it is the conscious action of men on the world, in Erich Fromm's words, 'as subject and agent of one's powers,' which is the source of their learning. In this regard, Arctic Gas' contention in its *Regional Socio-Economic Impact Statement* that the construction of a pipeline would raise the political consciousness of the Dene is particularly interesting. Consciousness-raising is implicit in true development, which is a process of conscious action and reflection. The proposed pipeline would only raise the consciousness of the Dene in the same sense that a man hit on the head with a hammer by another has a better idea of who his enemy is. The experience is hardly likely to be freely chosen in spite of such benefit!

Colonialism must be seen as an *experience*, and not simply a structural relationship. As such, it conditions both the colonizers and the colonized. A generation of Dene has now spent the better part of their young lives in colonial institutions, while a colonial system of government is well established even at the community level in the areas of housing, welfare, and settlement councils. This experience has been costly, breeding assumptions of cultural inferiority (or superiority) and eliciting racist analyses by both the white and Dene population. Only a thorough understanding of the nature of the colonial relationship and its opposition to human development will eliminate this legacy. Removal of colonial structures and their replacement by independent Dene institutions and the resources to make them effective will not, in itself, result in the elimination of the psychology of colonialism. This will take longer, and can only take place in a population which has experienced true development at an individual level, and has built into its work processes the ability to reflect on and understand the nature of such experience, so as better to institute such a process as a permanent feature of its social life.

Many Dene witnesses have clearly pointed out, in both the community hearings and the formal hearings of the Berger Inquiry, the relatively recent, but nevertheless substantial, intrusion on their lives of colonialism. The pipeline applicants have come to certain conclusions on the basis of data drawn from this colonial experience. Even if we were to accept the validity of their data (though in fact it is highly questionable), we have to recognize that any projection of the Dene future they made on the basis of a colonized past implies a continuation of colonialism. The Dene, on the other hand, have made it quite clear that their colonial experience was not of their choosing; nor can they accept its continuation into their future. The Dene assume a decolonized future supported by recognition of their political and property rights. What they seek to establish is a process of true development in place of colonial dehumanization.

Development is above all a process of shattering illusions which are the product of relations amongst men. Unless all parties to this debate are prepared to recognize the reality of their own conditioning and approach the arguments presented with that in mind, the outcome of both the pipeline issue and the aboriginal rights issue will be an imposed solution in the colonial tradition.

Who is really bound by tradition?

Reason may be applied to two essentially different purposes. First, it may be applied in the continuous elaboration and redefinition of reality as we experience it. Used in this way, reason turns its critical eye on everything. Nothing is given or taken for granted. This is reason in the service of human development. Reason at this level deals with such questions as the nature and purpose of man and what constitutes the good life.

Reason may be used in quite another way, as a designer or mechanic might use it to improve the workings of a machine whose existence he does not question. Within this limited framework, what is good or bad becomes defined in terms of what satisfies the need of the machine to work efficiently. The question of whether the machine serves the purpose of men or not need never be addressed if one views one's role simply as that of a mechanic, rather than more broadly as a member of the human race.

A society whose ideological underpinnings are no longer the object of other than 'academic' consideration, while its ideology demands reason merely in the service of efficiency, is a society out of control from any humanist perspective. Such a society is a prisoner of its ideology, defining men in terms of their fit with the ideological machine and, however much it claims to value individual freedom and enterprise, the truth is that it cannot afford non-conformity.

Describing such a society, the Canadian philosopher, George Grant, had this to say:

The old idea that 'the truth shall make you free,' that is, the view of reason as the way in which we discover the meaning of our lives and make that meaning our own, has almost entirely disappeared. In place of it we have substituted the idea of reason as a subjective tool, helping us in production, in the guidance of the masses, and in the maintenance of our power against rival empires ... I simply wish to emphasize that this philosophy, with its view of reason as an instrument, mirrors the actual life of our continent, in which individual freedom is subordinate to conformity.

Such an account of reason goes so deep into the modern consciousness that any other account is very difficult for a modern man to understand at all. Therefore, only by constant and relentless reflection on this modern idea can we hope to liberate ourselves from the naive acceptance of it.

Grant was not describing some vision of the future, but Canada of 1959. His description has become all the more accurate today. As our technology and advanced capitalist organization increasingly march to the tune of their own imperative, it becomes more and more difficult to accept their demands as reasonable. In fact, the use of the higher order of reason, which assesses reality in terms of human nature and purpose, becomes necessary to *our* survival, as well as the survival of the Dene.

Viewing the problem of colonialism from this perspective, as an ideological machine which has not only the Dene, but our society as a whole, in its grip, has the effect of turning many colonial ideas on their head. The suggestion that the Dene culture is 'traditional,' a thing of the past, becomes a joke. To one involved in the Dene struggle to assert their right to survive, it is quite clear that Canadian society, and the corporations whose imperative defines our choices, are the real 'traditionalists' today. The Dene proclaim a new future, while the oil companies and the federal government keep turning to the past. They are the ones to whom the phrase 'You cannot go back to your traditional ways' is truly applicable.

The process of human development

While both humanization and dehumanization are real alternatives, only the first is man's vocation. (Freire)

On various occasions the different parties involved in the debate over the issue of the proposed pipelines along the Mackenzie Valley have all attested to a desire to ensure that the development of the Dene and preservation of their culture would remain high on their list of priorities, should the pipeline be approved. Beyond this, both the government and the oil companies have argued that the project will, in fact, benefit the Dene, in spite of the latter's opposition to it, and notwithstanding some acknowledged cost in the realm of social disruption.

Although there has been an ill-informed suggestion at times that the Dene oppose 'development' the truth is that if one took the pronouncements of the pipeline applicants' and the government's intentions with regard to development and Dene culture and compared them with Dene pronouncements, there would appear to be little disagreement on the face of it. The reality, we know, is otherwise, and it is clear that the same words are used by the different parties in very different ways. Can we simply dismiss such confusion as being due to the 'subjective' nature of the problem? Can we say that it is simply a matter of opinion whether the pipeline will result in the development of the Dene and the continuation of Dene culture?

On the contrary, the meaning of development is, on reflection, quite precise and universally applicable. The effort to uncover the criteria according to which any change may be judged progressive or developmental, or regressive and dehumanizing, is essential if we are to take the discussion out of the realm of subjectivity where political power rather than reason may be allowed to define the issue.

The term 'development' has come to be used very loosely. While the purpose of human life is the development of mankind, the term 'development' has mostly lost contact with this human purpose and now refers mainly to quantitative or physical change, regardless of its relationship to the needs of men. The suggestion has even been made that the Dene oppose development, as if development were something that could be defined without reference to the Dene, something with a life of its own! The truth is that no healthy human being opposes *his own* development. On the contrary, all human beings, by nature, seek to develop.

Men develop themselves. They are not developed, or subject to development, by others. The word 'development' can only describe that *process* through which men develop. For example, a man cannot, as the saying goes, 'develop economically.' A corporation can, a mine can, but a man cannot be regarded as an *object* in the same sense without destroying what makes him a man, uniquely human. Men, rather than 'developing economically,' can meet their material needs in a manner which contributes to their development as men or in a manner which dehumanizes them.

What sets man apart? What is the essence of being human? And, of what, therefore, does the development of men consist?

What makes man human and unique is his ability for *conscious action* on his world – his ability to choose between alternative acts. Unlike the beaver, who for thousands of years has acted on his environment in precisely the same fashion, 'a man's life cannot "be lived" by repeating the pattern of his species; *he* must live ... Man is the only animal who finds his existence a problem which he has to solve and from which he cannot escape' (Fromm, 1955). Unlike the beaver, who exists in what Freire calls a 'one-dimensional today of which he has no consciousness,' man can perceive himself in the context of his own history, shaped by his past, but transcending it in his efforts to create his future.

Man's ability to develop, to become more human, in the sense of acting on his world with greater efficacy, derives from and is based on his critical capacity – his ability to reflect on and understand his experience, so as to inform his choices. Critical capacity depends on and breeds a sense of self-worth. It derives from a recognition that one's own experience is the source of understanding the world. To approach the world critically means to approach the world with man as the standard. This involves understanding that it is man who creates his own world, and that the act of creation is *the* human act. Conversely, this involves understanding that the creations of man cannot be permitted to become larger than man, in the sense of controlling him, demanding that he fit their specifications; for such is to rob him of his uniquely human capacity to develop himself, to make his own history.

The process of development can be seen as a continuous effort to address the contradiction between one's idea of reality and one's experience of reality. To the extent that we cling to one idea of reality and fight any threat to that idea, we become prisoners of our own creation and repress that which is most human in ourselves: our ability to transcend the given.

From this it is implicit that development is an internal process, of 'development out of' rather than 'development by.' Just as development cannot occur where one idea dominates us and stands between us and a better understanding of reality, so development cannot occur when someone else and their idea dominates us.

The process of human development, then, is a process where informed and conscious action leads to experience which, on critical reflection, leads to a new consciousness which once more expresses itself in action. Action - reflection - consciousness - choice, these are the essential ingredients of *being* human. Human existence is thus a process, a 'vocation' in Freire's words. That vocation can also be seen as the creation and recreation of man, the record of which is history and the expression of which is culture.

The colonial relationship

At the level of the individual, the essence of the colonial relationship may be understood in those situations where one individual is forced to relate to another on terms unilaterally defined by the other. The relationship is not negotiated, with each party having a say in its purpose. Where a contract exists, it merely states the terms under which one party virtually becomes the property of the other. The attitude of the colonialist to the colonized can best be appreciated as the attitude of a property owner to his property. Such colonial assumptions prevent the colonialist from accepting any move toward real autonomy on the part of the colonized. Any such move is either ignored, defined as unacceptable, or reprimanded, depending on the degree of institutionalization of the relationship. For example, the pipeline applicants assume that one issue for the Dene is whether they oppose or adapt to 'inevitable' change. This assumption completely ignores the possibility that the Dene do indeed favour change, but in this case, a change in the present colonial relationship which results in their facing, constantly, a future determined by others.

The assumption that change is defined and initiated unilaterally is itself characteristic of the colonialist mentality, natural in the context of the colonial relationship. It is, indeed, the pervading quality of *any* relationship where one party is used to making decisions for another. It affects the federal government approach to Indians, where the Dene are arguing for a change in the historical approach to aboriginal rights, from the destructive colonial interpretation imposed by the invading society to one which recognizes decolonization as its goal. But the assumption exists much more widely in our society. It is equally characteristic of bureaucratic relationships, both within bureaucracies and between bureaucracies and their so-called clients. All such relationships may be viewed as 'over-determined' by their colonial conditioning.

The behaviour of colonized men is prescribed behaviour – quite the opposite of what we have defined as the ideal of human existence – conscious action. We have defined human development as a process of action – reflection – consciousness – choice. The colonial relationship, however, is maintained by replacing human consciousness, which is the awareness of the human vocation of man as subject and creator of his world, with a colonial false-consciousness, with its dehumanized concept of man as object rather than subject of his world, and with its natural concomitants at the social level: racism and cultural superiority.

False consciousness, or 'selective inattention' as R.D. Laing calls it, 'as it becomes systematized, is ideology: the system of beliefs by which members of a social group ... develop a way of seeing, and interpreting what they see, congruent with what they have come to define as their interests: while denying, or providing no validation – perhaps even no language – for sensations that, if allowed to become perceptions and then ideas, would threaten those interests' (Friedenberg). It is this irrational, psychological aspect of colonial relationships which so often escapes our consciousness and which is the key to understanding the process of decolonization.

Van Ginkle Associates wrote a report for CAGPL and made colonialist change wholly determining:

The devaluation of the currency of the nation, a rise or a decline in the price of fur, a favourable or unfavourable shift in the balance of payments, a relevant technological breakthrough – the individual has no more capacity to alter those events than he has to halt the forward progress of a cruising space vehicle. As an individual the Mackenzie Valley inhabitant shares with his fellow citizens of the world an inability to control many of the events which may affect his life. And, equally, he shares an inability to halt change.

This study quotes approvingly a remark of Benjamin Disraeli (why Disraeli?) to the effect that 'change is inevitable.' Nothing more. This mindless platitude, devoid of qualitative content, typifies the fatalism of colonial false-conscious-

ness. A truly human consciousness is critical, and implicit in it is the awareness of choice between humanizing and dehumanizing alternatives. Consciousness devoid of its implication for man's ability to humanize (change) his circumstances is meaningless.

The Van Ginkle study goes on to suggest that the Dene share with their
fellow men an inability to exercise control over the changes they experience
or will experience in future. Choice it would seem is non-existent. Adaptation
is their only vocation. No argument could better represent the choice posed
by this pipeline than that put forward by those Darwinists-in-reverse, the Van
Ginkles. The choice is quite simply between a future which recognizes the
uniquely human possibility of development (action – reflection – consciousness – choice) or a future which condemns men to the experience of the
beaver. The Van Ginkle argument must be seen for what it is – a mere rationalization for dehumanization.

The kind of illogical conclusions these assumptions lead one to, may be
seen from these further remarks in the Van Ginkle study:

The extent and the nature of the impact of any event may also depend upon
the manner in which the community adjusts or accommodates – on the resili-
ence of the people and the capacity of the community to turn the resultants
of an action to its own advantage ... In the final analysis the impact of any
event depends in large measure on the determination to maximize new oppor-
tunities. The event, of itself, does not dictate whether advantage or disadvantage will accrue to the people and community; this is dictated by the reaction
to the event.

Could there be a more perfect example of colonial thought, a more obvious
abdication of responsibility, than the ludicrous suggestion that a community
is responsible for the outcome of decisions over which it has no control? One
person on reading this passage wryly referred to it as the 'Hiroshima theory,'
according to which those we have come to view as victims of the bomb simply reacted inappropriately!

The fact that such an argument could be put forward seriously gives us a
further insight into the nature of consciousness. It is only in a colonial world
that such a suggestion could be made. Consciousness is bred of experience. It
is natural, therefore, that the colonialist consciousness, bred of a dehumanizing relationship, should exhibit dehumanizing assumptions.

While the short-term material interest of those who support the applicants' proposal is served by such rationalization, the long-term interests of
these same people as human beings can only be met by a change in the colonial relationship. The efforts of the Dene to decolonize themselves will eventually lead to such a change of consciousness in the direction of humanization

on the part of those who prepared the Van Ginkle study. And this will be true for the consciousness of Canadians in general, hitherto bred of a dehumanizing relationship to aboriginal people in the country as a whole.

Culture, history and colonialism

Who controls the past controls the future. And who controls the present controls the past. (Orwell)

An understanding of what culture really is would seem essential since not only the Dene but also the federal government and the applicants have argued that the preservation of Dene culture is something they support. Let me simply say that culture lives in men, not in museums. It is what people *do* together. The preservation of Dene culture implies, necessarily, recognition of the way the Dene define themselves. Only the Dene can define their culture, and Dene culture is alive today to the extent that the Dene announce their own identity. For this reason, the united Dene struggle for recognition of their rights is every bit as much a cultural act as making a skin boat or holding a drum dance. Dene culture will exist as long as there are people who define themselves as Dene, and Dene culture will be what they do together.

It is the shared experience from conscious, united action which makes Dene culture a living reality. Anyone who thinks culture is represented simply by artifacts and dying rituals is a prisoner of colonial consciousness. This is true because it is characteristic of a colonial relationship that it deprives men of their sense of themselves, today, relegating their identity to a thing of the past. Only consciously active men have a culture and a history that defines them.

To quote Amilcar Cabral:

it is not possible to harmonize the economic and political domination of a people, whatever may be the degree of their social development, with the preservation of their cultural personality.

and Freire:

There is no history *without* men and no history *for* men; there is only history *of* men, made by men and in turn making them. It is when ... majorities are denied their right to participate in history as subjects that they become dominated and alienated ... to supersede their condition as objects by the status of subjects requires that the people *act*, as well as reflect, upon the reality to be transformed.

Colonial men do not act autonomously. They must be satisfied with the illusion of acting through the actions of others. They merely perform a role defined for them in someone else's game plan. In this sense, they are men without history. Since history is the creation of consciously active men, those whose behaviour is prescribed cannot be said to be making their own history. Colonialism is, thus, the theft of human history. To understand this is to understand that the first act on the part of a colonized person or group to decolonize themselves is itself a return to the human vocation of making history.

A telling example of colonialism as the negation of history can be found in the erasure of Dene place-names throughout the Mackenzie District, and their replacement by those of the colonialists. Faced daily with such crude misnomers as that of the Mackenzie River, the Dene suffer a constant implicit denigration of their own past, and a suggestion that the future is not theirs to announce. Perhaps the most serious example is the negation of thousands of years of democratic experience on the part of the Dene exemplified by the presumptuous imposition of alien political institutions.

It should be clear from the foregoing why colonialism has been described as the theft of history. Equally, it should be clear why colonialism is incompatible with the continuation and preservation of Dene culture. Those who truly support the latter objective will recognize colonialism as *the* problem and work to overcome it. This will be the test of their sincerity.

From all we have said, it should go without saying that the development process we have outlined as the uniquely human possibility cannot be instituted in a world where the present and future are determined by forces outside of the community, or outside of the individuals who compose it. Quite simply, political control, giving men the freedom to determine their relationships and the work they will choose to do together, is implicit in the process of human development. The ability to reflect on one's circumstances is useless if the political capacity to redirect the course of development in one's community is absent.

The Dene demand for recognition of political rights is nothing more or less than recognition that this is an essential enabling element in their own development and in the continuation of their culture and history.

Colonial relations in bureaucracies

The colonial relationship is not limited to relationships between cultures, as we have already stated. It is the pattern of relationships within bureaucracies in general. It is the nature of colonialism to reward those who show a readiness to subsume their own true interest, that is, the development of themselves as autonomous creative human beings, to the requirements of an external purpose. Those who serve give up the discovery of their human potency in exchange for security and the vicarious sharing in the power of the bureaucracy itself, whatever purpose it serves.

Here is how Daniel Ellsberg came to understand the readiness of bureaucrats to serve the purposes of others:

> There are two parts to the message they hear: one part is, by *yourself*, you're powerless. The other side is: if you join up, you can share in their power, you can plug in. The power will flow through you; at least you'll be part of it. That double notion has a very great coercive effect in itself. It makes people terrified of the idea of being cut off from that machine. It's a kind of fear, a social control, that does not merely mean, 'I'm going to have trouble finding a job if I lose this one,' or, 'What will my friends say?,' but an emotional vague, gut fear, horror at the idea of being cut off ... Those men have a self-image of powerlessness except as loyal servants not of the constitution, not of their countrymen, not of humanity, but of the man who hired them. (Terkel 1973)

What Ellsberg is describing is the dynamics of colonial relationships and as such could be applied with little or no alteration to any number of colonial situations.

Colonialism is not simply a Dene problem; it is our problem.

The stability of bureaucracy, in spite of its dehumanizing nature, can only be understood in terms of its ability to remove from those who work within it the sense of responsibility for the purpose to which they contribute. Similarly, the absence of critical consciousness can be understood, first, as being essential to the maintenance of an authoritarian structure which exploits the energy of many for the purposes of few, and second, as essential to the sanity and security of those who seek to avoid the truth of their own responsibility, their own humanity.

Let me quote here a famous bureaucrat, who had many years in prison to reflect on how he was able to evade responsibility for the purposes he served, Albert Speer:

> The ordinary party member was being taught that grand policy was much too complex for him to judge it. Consequently, one felt one was being represented, never called upon to take personal responsibility. The whole structure of the system was aimed at preventing conflicts of conscience from even arising.

However, Speer also recognized that

> If I was isolated, I determined the degree of my own isolation. If I was ignorant, I ensured my own ignorance. If I did not see, it was because I did not want to see.

It is necessary to emphasize the dehumanizing aspect of the colonial relationship on those who serve the colonialist interest in order to bring home the point that the so-called 'social impact' of colonial development must be recognized as affecting all those involved and not simply those who oppose colonial interests.

The task of decolonization

The idea of consciousness is more complicated yet. If a colonial relationship conditions and determines the consciousness of those involved, how does decolonization come about? It would be relatively easy to answer that since men have the capacity to reflect on the fact of their conditioning they are then able to transcend such conditioning in the direction of liberation. This is, of course, true, but does not account for the reality of the continuation and stability of the colonial relationships which permeate our society. Clearly, relationships of dependency, unhealthy and destructive though they may be to the human beings involved, derive their strength from strong irrational and unconscious impulses on both sides.

In a society where such relationships are the general rule, as in a colonial society, the man who accepts the challenge of his own freedom has to face the fear of tremendous loneliness, isolation, and the experience of the outsider. Shouldering responsibility for one's own self in a bureaucratic world, where institutions appear to serve chiefly the function of relieving men of the burden of responsibility in the name of a higher authority, is a challenge few have the courage to accept, in the North or in the country as a whole. It is in this context that the Dene assertion of nationhood must be understood as providing the collective support and the mobilizing idea needed in facing the challenge of freedom.

Overemphasis on structural change, while ignoring the intractable, irrational, and psychological aspects of dependency, serves only the cause of dehumanization. This is so because the process of development is mystified, and the exploitative relationships continue under a new guise. Such is the nature of neo-colonialism. Perhaps the best examples of this are recent land settlements, like the Alaska Settlement, which have ignored the development process and have imposed structures on aboriginal people totally alien to their experience, such as 'development corporations.' Such land settlements are truly colonialism in a different costume.

It is here that the expectation on the part of the federal government that the Dene should be able to respond, as if to a questionnaire, with a detailed description of a 'land claim' so thoroughly misses the point. The Dene have announced their intention to decolonize themselves. They have also insisted that a land settlement must make real development, Dene development, a possibility. They are much more realistic than the federal government when they recognize that their first task will be to come to terms with their colonial experience in a long-term effort to rebuild their nation on the principles of non-exploitative development. When the nature of colonialism as a relationship and an experience is fully grasped, the unreality of expecting, today, of a colonized people a complete blueprint for their decolonization, should be evident.

The first task for the Dene, and one that takes a great deal of time and effort, is to identify and discard colonial conditioning, that element of their identity *prescribed* by the colonial relationship. Then, armed with a more authentic definition of their interests, the Dene will be in a position to plan the course of their own development.

To quote Erich Fromm once more:

modern man lives under the illusion that he knows that he wants, while he actually wants what he is *supposed* to want. In order to accept this it is necessary to realize that to know what one really wants is not comparatively easy, as most people think, but one of the most difficult problems any human being has to solve. It is a task we frantically try to avoid by accepting ready-made goals as though they were our own. Modern man is ready to take great risks when he tries to achieve the aims which are supposed to be 'his,' but he is deeply afraid of taking the risk and the responsibility of giving himself his own aims. (Fromm, 1941)

What the Dene are setting out to accomplish is no mean task and will entail a struggle within their own community long after the struggle with non-Dene society is resolved. Recognition of the necessity for this struggle is difficult for any Canadians who have not come to terms with the colonial problem in their lives, let alone for those whose short-term interest is served by the continuation of colonial relations. Yet understanding the nature of the Dene rights position depends on an understanding of the colonial relationship and its legacy of conditioning. What the Dene are really demanding is not so much an aboriginal right but a human right, the right to undertake decolonization – or as it may be understood in a positive sense, the right to develop.

Colonialism and decolonization: the example of language

The nature of colonialism and the key to decolonization can be elucidated by examining the area of language. Man, in the process of human existence, puts his unique stamp on the world around him. His culture, at any point of time, embodying all that he creates, both in the realm of physical change and in the realm of institutions, ideas, and language, exhibits his understanding of himself and his world. These products of man's conscious activity constitute his vocabulary, broadly defined. His development derives from his consciousness of this vocabulary and from his efforts to transcend or redefine it in the light of his experience. It stands to reason, then, that for development to occur, this vocabulary must be integral to the men concerned. It must be theirs. Under colonialism such development is impossible since the terms of the vocabulary are prescribed from without.

A lengthy colonial experience not only deprives people of their right to define their experience authentically, but even deprives them of consciousness of such a right. This describes why so much that is vital to the human experience of development is, under colonialism, defined as the realm of the 'other.'

In embarking on a course of development and decolonization, the Dene have begun to reject the prescribed colonial language in favour of terms which fit their experience and new consciousness of their relationship to the world. To describe the world is the human function. Men can only describe *their* world through the use of words *they* create or 'own.' Words do not, of themselves, have this ability. For example, the word 'progress' does not describe the same kind of change for all men in a colonial world. What is considered progress by some may be oppression for others. Words are like tools and must serve the purposes of men, and not the reverse. In a colonial relationship between oppressor and oppressed, the same word cannot serve the purpose of both colonialist and colonized since their experiences and interests differ. In the ideal democratic and egalitarian society, the imposition of definitions becomes impossible, while under colonialism the majority have lost their right to 'name the world' (Freire).

The act of reasserting one's right to define the world, as exemplified by the Dene Declaration, is naturally upsetting to those whose short-term interest is served by the continuation of colonial prescription and exploitation. Adverse reactions to efforts of the Dene to describe their experience in a more authentic terminology must be judged in the light of the disintegration of the colonial relationship. The power of those who are used to naming the world for others is being *undermined*, and the reaction is defensive.

Look at the words, 'land claims.' Anyone familiar with the way the Dene view their land would understand that this term in no way characterizes what they conceive of as the struggle for their rights. The term suggests that the federal government in fact holds all the land by right and the Dene wish to claim some of it. Not only does this misrepresent the Dene concept of land, but it totally ignores the element of political rights so vital to the decolonization of the Dene.

Insistence on a colonial definition of the Dene rights struggle precludes the possibility of decolonizing the Dene through negotiation. Unless the nature of the colonial relationship is grasped at this fundamental level, the Dene will be left with the colonial non-choice of 'negotiating the extinguishment of their rights.' 'Negotiating the extinguishment of rights' is a phrase which is ludicrous outside the context of a colonial relationship. The Dene at the community level have long struggled with trying to comprehend *why*, if they have these rights, 'negotiation' is even required.

Alexis Arrowmaker, former Chief of the Dogribs, makes this quite clear when he says:

Indian people have their own society in which their relationship to land is crucial. The meaning of ownership is very important to this Indian idea. Cabinet ministers do not understand this Indian concept or the way we see ourselves in relation to this land. They are stuck inside their own society and concepts, and they try to impose their view on us. We cannot compromise because it means giving up our concept and accepting theirs. We are not talking only about land, but also about Dene people and how we see ourselves as a group.

A leadership seeking to decolonize the Dene must define the struggle in only one way, a struggle for recognition. A leadership prepared to accept a neocolonial solution can entertain the concept of 'extinguishing rights,' but if they do so they cannot involve their own people in any conscious way in such an exercise. This is so because no man, through negotiation, will consciously extinguish his right to *be*. The colonialist tends to view as unrepresentative any leadership which questions the colonial relationship. However, the only representative leadership in the sense of representing the interests of the Dene as human beings must view decolonization as *the* issue.

The experience of colonialism is an experience of alienation. The fact that the term 'land claims' does not define the Dene conception of their situation (which they conceive as a situation where their rights as a people are being ignored) has more practical ramifications. As long as the term continues to be used by the Dene themselves they are left in the paradoxical situation of having someone versed in non-Dene concepts define its meaning! It is not unusual for some Dene to demand of their own leaders that they explain 'what land claims is.' The people who ask such advice are not unable to define their own position, but *are* unable to understand and 'own' someone else's definition. What could be more natural? This is, in a nutshell, the essence of colonialism – a relationship which leaves one side dependent on the other to define the world. An unscrupulous leadership could exploit the situation if it were prepared to accept the colonial definition of the problem. This could be the outcome, of course, if the federal government remains unyielding in its demands that the Dene present a 'land claims position' on its terms, and refuse to consider seriously what the Dene are really saying.

Conclusion

The Dene cannot afford to take colonialism for granted, nor can anyone. To do so will be to add impetus to an ideological and institutional machine which oppresses and dehumanizes all.

The connection between the Dene struggle and the problem of development which confronts us all is obvious when we see our development as a problem of overcoming the false-consciousness of alienation. The alienated state is characterized by an acceptance of situations where what is merely man-made, whether it be a machine or an idea, word, or institution, acquires a power of its own which is exercised against man and the authority of which he accepts. The implication of such a situation is that men have lost sight of their power to create and change their world, and that exercising this uniquely human trait is the source of their development. Failure to exercise this potentiality is to accept dehumanization and to be alienated.

Therefore, it must be understood that the kind of land settlement the Dene are talking about not only involves structural recognition of the political right to decide what takes place on Dene land, but also involves a process of decolonization, which is the more arduous and difficult to institute the longer the Dene experience colonialism (and the larger the colonial establishment becomes). In both these senses, therefore, the construction of the proposed pipeline, before recognition of the rights of the Dene, is a prime example of colonialism since it will certainly prejudice both the political rights they demand and the process of decolonization which is the only process which merits the term 'development.'

Perhaps most important of all, the value of examining the nature of the colonial relationship is evident from the light it sheds on the Dene rights or, as some call it, 'land claims' issue. Unless both the colonized and the colonialist take the time to examine how each of their views are conditioned by the colonial relationship they will continue to carry on what has been called 'un dialogue des sourdes' – a dialogue of the deaf. This is so because it is inherent in colonial relations that one side does the talking while the other is to all intents and purposes presumed to be mute.

REFERENCES

Cabral, Amilcar, *Return to the Source: Selected Speeches of Amilcar Cabral*
    (New York, 1973)
Canadian Arctic Gas Pipeline Ltd., *Regional Socio-Economic Impact Statement* (1974);
    Communities of the Mackenzie: Effects of the Hydrocarbon Industry (a study
    prepared for Arctic Gas by Van Ginkle Associates Ltd., 1975)

Freire, Paulo, *Pedagogy of the Oppressed* (New York, 1972)

Friedenberg, E.Z., *Laing* (London, 1973)

Fromm, Erich, *Escape from Freedom* (New York, 1941); *The Sane Society* (New York, 1955)

Grant, George, *Philosophy in the Mass Age* (Toronto, 1959)

Orwell, George, *1984* (London, 1949)

Speer, Albert, *Inside the Third Reich* (New York, 1971)

Terkel, Studs, 'Servants of the State' (A Conversation with Daniel Ellsberg) *Harpers* (1973)

The Political System and the Dene

George Barnaby

George Kurszewski

Gerry Cheezie

GEORGE BARNABY

The land claim of the Dene is a claim not only for land but also for political rights. Up to this time the native people have had no say in what happens on their land. Everything has been decided by Ottawa or a few people in Yellowknife. This does not apply to development on the land only, but also in the way we live. Laws are made by people from the south that do not make sense to us, but which we have to live by. These laws are to serve the system of the south. They are not laws to protect the Dene way of life.

The land claim is our fight to gain recognition as a different group of people – with our own way of seeing things, our own values, our own life style, our own laws.

The land claim is a fight for self-determination using our own system with which we have survived till now. This system is based on community life. Whether it be a settlement or a trapping camp, whether people live by working in a wage economy or off the land, the laws we follow are concerned with all the people, not to benefit a few at the expense of the rest. Sharing with others is one of our laws. People are expected to share. The ones that have a lot always share with the rest of the people. A person will never have to go hungry, for instance, as other people will give what they could spare. A person who could afford an outboard motor or skidoo helps someone who needs help to move out in the bush.

Respect for the old people is another law, since all the laws come from the teaching by our elders. From stories that give us pride in our culture, from training since we are young, we learn what is expected of us. Without this learning from the elders our culture will be destroyed.

The way decisions are made is another law. No one can decide for another person, everyone is involved in a discussion, and the decision made by everyone. Our way is to try and give freedom to a person, as he knows what he wants. When working, for instance, a person should not be forced into anything. Supposing he wants to go trapping for a while, the system should be flexible enough to allow this. There should be a choice.

Our life is part of the land. We live on the land and are satisfied with what we get from it. No one person owns land, it belongs to all of us. We choose where we want to go and our choice is respected by others whether in the settlement or in the bush. We have no word in our language that means wilderness, as anywhere we go is our home. It does not make sense to destroy your home. People love to live in the bush; it is a part of our culture.

These are a few examples of the culture of the Dene, the system of government, the laws, the way they differ from the southern system and people. The Territorial Council, from which I recently resigned, is one place where Dene law is not respected at all. There is very little involvement by the people; the laws that are passed have no importance for the people, but they are forced to follow these laws. The whole system is from the south, and they are trying to fit us into it.

A lot of times the topics that are being discussed are not understood by all the councillors. The effects of passing laws are not understood. The language that is used is not understood. The procedures and formality is confusing; most of the time, rather than look stupid, we just agree. As most of these discussions concern only the southerners, if they choose to live that way, it is up to them.

The first session of Council I went to, we spent two weeks on an ordinance that had no importance to the people I represented. At this time I asked for more control for the communities. This was voted down. I don't know why. Since the Territories is a big land and people want different things in different places, one thing it might have done was reduce the size of the territorial government, as people would do more of the planning and carrying out of programs for themselves. But even if we all agreed, the final decision is up to the Commissioner of the NWT or the Department of Indian and Northern Affairs.

At the second session of Council we talked of political development, where the Council would have authority over the whole north. I spoke against this, as it would make no difference to the people; it still would not give them any rights to decide for themselves. The power would be only to the Council to decide the future of the North, and people would be forced to follow, whether they agreed or not. I think it was a plan to keep the people oppressed. We would get a land claim, but live under the laws of some one who has no concern for us or our wishes or our own laws.

In January 1976 we went through the budgets for the territorial government. This budget was prepared by the territorial government and approved in Ottawa. We could not change any money from one program to another. All we could do was take it or leave it. We approved everything. At this time two motions were made regarding the pipeline. The first was the pipeline authority

– that the Council should have input into this body. I argued at this time that the people concerned should have the control if there was to be any authority since they would be affected the most. This was brushed aside with the remark that no group should control the pipeline. So if the concern was not for the people of the north, I don't know what it was. Second was that the Council support the building of the pipeline down the Mackenzie Valley. Here was a real example of oppression. Since the people had already stated their position against this project, the Council was not speaking for them. What they wanted to do was to put down the stand against the pipeline. I don't know what the people from the Eastern Arctic were thinking when they voted in support, as they have no idea what is happening here. I would think as native people they would share the same concern for people that we do. What I said was that if they wanted a pipeline they could approve it on their own land, but not force it on us. But I hope they did not understand the whole issue and what it means to us.

At this time there were remarks made about the Berger Inquiry that would make it look foolish, but I believe it is the first chance that people have had to really speak their mind. But apparently the Council does not want that; they don't want anyone speaking for themselves. They want to decide everything.

Sometimes I say, that if the commissioner and the top executives of the territorial government were all trappers and hunters things would be different, but I see it would make no difference. It is the system which is wrong: wherever only a few people decide for the rest of the population, it oppresses people.

Some people might think of the land claim as a racial issue, but it really is an issue between the ruled and the rulers, between the oppressed and the oppressors. Under Dene law there is freedom and equality. The system from the south is oppression and exploitation, where a few have a lot and a lot of people have very little.

Where the Dene work together in time of need, the southern way is to exploit that need. Where the Dene share, only profit moves people in the southern system. Where the Dene law gives freedom for the individual to do what he decides and take responsibility for his action, the system from the south passes an ordinance which forces a person's action and takes away responsibility. Where our system is set up to serve the people, the people from the south serve their system.

The Dene Declaration clearly states that we are a nation of people with our own ways of governing ourselves, our own values, and life style. The land claim is our fight to survive as a nation and to decide our own future.

GEORGE KURSZEWSKI AND GERRY CHEEZIE

The land claim that the Dene of the Northwest Territories are making is not just a claim for recognition of Dene aboriginal title to the land but also a claim for recognition of political rights that are now being ignored by federal and territorial governments. To illustrate the 'political genocide' that is happening in the north today, and to give you an idea of how political structures are imposed on us in a way that destroys our own community structures, we're going to use Fort Smith as an example. Fort Smith is a community that we're familiar with, and a community where we have tried to work within the system. We want to describe the experience we've had and the conclusions to which that experience leads us.

Fort Smith is the southernmost community in the Northwest Territories, situated about a half mile above the Alberta border. It's made up of approximately 2800 people. Approximately 1600 of them are Dene, and 1200 are white people. This gives us approximately a 60 per cent native majority. The governing body that has been set up in Fort Smith to make local decisions was created not by the people of Fort Smith, but by the territorial government through its municipal ordinance. It has been designed particularly for the population of Fort Smith that have moved from southern Canada to Fort Smith. It's designed in a way that these people from southern Canada can get onto the municipal council and take part in it much more readily than the native population can.

As we see the municipal council and the political structure that is set up, it pretends to represent the community, but literally does not represent the community. It's made along the lines of southern thinking. This type of political structure would fit well into a southern community where people give the power to decide what happens to their community to eight or nine people. So the minority of the population is familiar with this type of structure; however, the majority of the population is not familiar with it and does not agree with the whole concept on which the structure is based. The native majority do not believe that eight or nine people should decide the future of the community. They believe that the future of the community should be decided by the community, by the long-term residents who are the native people and the white people who have decided that they want to make Fort Smith their home and have an interest in the community other than a monetary one.

We would like to outline some experiences we've had with the present political structure. The best example we can give is that of the municipal council elections that were held on 8 December 1975 in Fort Smith, where the native people tried to become part of the governmental system there.

The council is made up of eight councillors and one mayor. Four of these positions were open on 8 December. Six native people ran for these positions and five white people ran. There were eleven contenders for the four councillor positions, and when the outcome of the elections were reached, three white people were elected to the Council and one native person.

Even though the native people of Fort Smith make up 60 per cent of the population, they did not come out to vote. There were a lot of problems in the election because a lot of the native people couldn't understand the procedure that was being carried out. A lot of the native population did not show up at the polling stations because this is not their way of deciding the future of their community. Native people do not go the polls once a year to elect someone to decide their own future. The way the Dene of Fort Smith would much rather decide things is through a structure that is set up by the people themselves and that will meet their interest, the interest of the long-term residents, the interest of the majority, instead of the interest of the minority and the transient population.

The outcome of the December election, where one native person got on Council, was a real discouragement to the native people of Fort Smith who wanted to try to participate within the present political structure. They saw that there was little hope that they could take effective part in it. They could not get the proper representation on the municipal council, because it is a foreign system. Municipal council is not the way in which the native community of Fort Smith wishes to have the future of the community decided. It is not the political structure within which they would like to decide their own future.

The situation in Fort Smith shows why the Indian Brotherhood of the Northwest Territories and the Metis Association of the Northwest Territories have said 'no major development before a land settlement.' The people who are making decisions about development are not the people who should be deciding these things. The core of the community is not involved in the decision-making process there. The majority is not involved in deciding what goes on. The different projects that are proposed for around Fort Smith and that area are being looked at by eight or nine people, and the decisions should not be made by these people.

That's why we're saying that there should be no major developments before a land settlement. Our rights to decide our own future through our own political institutions must be recognized first, so that we'll be able to take an effective part in the future of the North and be able to survive as a people.

GEORGE KURSZEWSKI

Let me give another example of how decisions made by the people involved in the present political structures are often contrary to the way the native people of Fort Smith would like to see things happen. The Northern Roads Commission came around to the communities to find out what it was the people thought about the proposed road systems, and the Town Council at that time came out with a brief and presented it to the Northern Roads Commission stating that the people of Fort Smith wanted a road to Fort McMurray, and wanted a dam on the Slave River, and this was presented by the Council which said that it represented the people of Fort Smith.

What we are saying is that when decisions of this nature or projects of this nature are proposed, it should not be a council or a system that is foreign to the people that makes the decision about whether or not projects like this should go ahead or not. We feel that when projects are proposed that affect the future of our community, that affect the future of ourselves as a people, that we should be involved in this.

And when the Town Council presented its brief to the Northern Roads Commission, we had not been consulted. There was no public meeting. There was no effort at all on behalf of the local government system there to find out whether the people of Fort Smith really wanted to have a road coming in from the south and a dam on the Slave River. There was no effort to do this.

And these are the type of decisions that we see being made every day that are affecting our lives and planning our own future. And we feel that this shouldn't go on any further, that before any type of development goes ahead, like the road to McMurray and a dam on the Slave River, the people should be guaranteed their political security to decide what happens to themselves, instead of the authority to decide these things lying in the hands of a few people and a foreign system.

There's a name change that has just gone on recently with the Metis population in Smith. The Metis people have changed the structure of their organization and have called it, to begin with, the Fitz-Smith Metis Community. It will include all the people who live around the area and representation in our organization will be based on family units. This means that the council will be made up of all the families represented. This is how we wish to decide things about our own future and our own organization, through a structure or a system that the people themselves have formed – a structure that people believe in.

I think this has been the history of native people, that no one should decide the future of any other person, that everyone should be involved in deciding what happens in a community, and that a few people should not decide for the rest.

This is what the people in Fort Smith are attempting to put across to the rest of the population and this is what we are emphasizing most in our land claim, that we must be guaranteed the political security that is rightfully ours to decide our own future through our own political institutions, not through a foreign system of any kind, but through institutions that the people themselves develop to meet their own needs. And this is why we emphasize that no development take place until this right of native people is recognized by the federal government. This is what we are after.

GERRY CHEEZIE

The biggest thing which I would like to talk about right now would be the big gap between how territorial and local governments see their kind of government as suitable for the people, and how we see our own government as being suitable for our needs, and trying to show the gap that lies between these two things. An example is that election we had in Fort Smith.

There's a lot of reasons why we failed. The biggest one of all is that the people do not understand this kind of system. You are talking to hunters and trappers, people living from the land. A lot of other people say that we don't have any system of government, that we don't know what we are doing.

I disagree and 60 per cent of the people in Smith disagree, because there is no way that we are being given any kind of fair responsibility to try to solve some of the problems ourselves. I think if the choice was given to the people now, we would go ahead and operate under a system which we ourselves would develop, not something that is imposed on us by a territorial government and by the federal government or the oil companies, or whoever is doing it.

I don't believe that any kind of development is going to help this situation at all. And with the Mackenzie Valley pipeline project, the way I see it, the communities down the Mackenzie will experience the kind of things that happened in Smith. Fort Smith has become a community where people stay for a large part of their lives now; they have been moved into the community from the bush away from their hunting and trapping lifestyle.

I don't see any hope for those people. There is no way that you can tell an old trapper, an old man, that he doesn't have a system of this own, that he can't voice his concerns just because he can't write up a piece of paper and can't communicate effectively except in his native language.

There is no way that can happen. I think the only way that the people can survive here is if they are given the time to develop their own kind of system which they can operate themselves, which would give respect to the kind of culture they have, to the lifestyle and the environment and the land that the Dene people are trying to recover from the government.

We ran six candidates in that election in Fort Smith for the four seats and we had difficulty running this kind of a scheme because a lot of people didn't understand that they had to vote four times on one slate. On some of the ballots, there was only one 'X' where there were supposed to be four. And we had gone through a lesson, I guess you could call it, with these people telling them, this is how to vote; telling, explaining to them clearly that they had four votes each. But a lot of the people took only one vote, so we lost a lot of votes like that. And that just goes to show that this kind of system doesn't work for people up here and it won't ever work, so I think we should sit down now and try to change it.

These people have concerns that are those of 60 per cent of the population in that town, and they have no control over anything. If they wanted to build houses somewhere, they couldn't build houses because there's municipal by-laws which are passed. They say you can't put up a structure unless it meets certain criteria; and those are all tied and interrelated. Then the people come to me as the chief of the band and say, 'Well, can I build a house here?' And I say, 'Go ahead. Build it wherever you want. It is your land.' But they come around later and say the Town Council says they will take you to court if you build a house on that land, or if they went through the Municipal Council route they have come across a bylaw which stopped them from building a home there.

These are the kind of things which I believe don't respect our concerns at all. They don't make any room for them.

I guess it all comes down to the land claim. It is the only thing that can ensure the survival of our people. There has to be a political settlement. They have to recognize our rights to develop our own institutions, not something that's imposed. There's no way the people up here can survive if the federal government or the oil companies go ahead and build that pipeline without giving the Dene people in the Territories the right to decide for themselves the things concerning their lives.

The way I see things, it'll destroy them. Look at the case in Smith; that community is going on its second hundred years, and over the first hundred years I don't think the governmental system gave any room for the people there to develop in any way at all. I grew up in Fort Smith; even my parents, I tried to get them out to vote; and my mother, I sat down with her and told her: 'You got four votes. Make sure, you know, you vote for the people that would represent our concerns.' And she only voted for one candidate. That probably happened a hundred times, even more. We figured we had a good chance because we had 60 per cent of the population, but we figure now that numbers alone don't make any advantage. It works beautifully theoretically, but we're talking about something that these people don't know anything about. It makes no sense to them.

The town council system doesn't leave any room for us to participate, because it steadily undermines my authority as chief of the band. What they're telling me in effect is that I have no say at all in that community.

We're not asking for special status. We're just asking for what's rightfully ours, that nobody ever bothered to discuss with us. We're undergoing a change up here; it's happening very quickly. We're trying to work under all these pressures, trying to prepare people, trying to make them understand that if we don't do something now, if the government doesn't pay heed to our position, that all these things we're talking about are meaningless, that we're going to be wiped out anyway.

The kind of things that we see as important to our survival are being totally disregarded by going ahead and building the pipeline. I don't see any way at all that the pipeline can help towards the betterment of the natives in the Territories. If anything at all, it's going to destroy them.

It just goes to show, like the situation in Smith which has been there for a hundred years, that the situation of the native people there has deteriorated all within that time and in my experience there has been no respect given to the people that were living there, to the kind of things that they were concerned about; their hunting and trapping rights, the places they could live.

If the government doesn't realize our concerns they can wipe us out. That's why it is really important to realize that the land claim is not just for a few rights to hunt in a certain area. Not around the pipeline, or something to that effect. We want to make it quite clear that we want to see a land claims settlement before the pipeline goes ahead because there's no way that we can participate as equal partners if that doesn't happen.

I myself find it very hard to operate under the government system which doesn't give me any authority to do anything at all. They say the Fort Smith Town Council has the power in Fort Smith; and here I am, the chief, and George and myself, representing 60 per cent of the population with no say over anything.

People in my band come to me and ask for explanations of why certain things are happening in the community, and I try to explain to them that the Town Council is the only body in that town which is recognized by the territorial government and by the federal government or other large corporations that want to deal within that town. If an oil company came into town, it certainly wouldn't deal with us. It deals with the Town Council because that's the legitimate government body, and it totally disregards the majority of the people by doing that.

One of the problems my people have when they try to participate in the system the way it is now, is the language barrier. To go back to the election, everything was in English and the language predominately in Smith right now is Chipewyan. Even myself – I'm a high school graduate – I still can't talk the language. I find it hard understanding different meanings to different words because it has one meaning in a different context and, take it out of that one, it has a totally different meaning; and when we're talking or we're trying to explain something like a municipal ordinance to people like this, how do you explain those differences? In our language, there's no distinction like that.

All of this just goes to show that there's no consideration made by the people who institute this system on us. They give us no right at all to decide anything for ourselves.

Colonialism in the Communities

Wilf Bean

When I came north to work for the government of the Northwest Territories in 1968, the movement of the native people from traditional hunting camps to centralized settlements was just being completed in the Central Arctic. In the brief orientation session which the previous area administrator of Cambridge Bay had with me, he related his success at finally convincing the Perry Island people to move into Cambridge Bay. It was because he had taken the trouble to travel to Perry River by dog team, my predecessor told me, that he had been able to convince a family to relocate to Cambridge Bay. He had also made it clear to them that only in Cambridge Bay would government housing and 'rations' be available. There too, the family could be together with the children who were in grade school. As my predecessor saw it, it was his success at convincing the last remaining family group to move to the settlement that was primarily responsible for his promotion to a new position in the regional office. In retrospect, the move from camps to centralized settlements had great significance for the native peoples, not the least of which was the establishment of the dominance of the government and the reciprocal dependency of native peoples.

The previous area administrator also briefed me on the then advisory council that operated in the settlements. There was a need to co-ordinate activities within each settlement and the advisory council meetings were useful to keep everyone informed of each other's activities. As I found out later, membership on the Cambridge Bay Advisory Council was typical of most other settlements. There were representatives from each federal agency in the community – the RCMP corporal, the NCPC (Northern Canada Power Commission) manager, the head nurse, the MOT airport manager, the school principal, representatives from each church, the Bay manager, the private business enterprises, and the area administrator.

Discussion centred around mutual administrative concerns: the nurse asking the RCMP to shoot some loose dogs; the Bay manager asking the administrator to guarantee an advance for someone to go hunting; the local entrepreneur asking the NCPC manager if there would be money for a contract to build an addition to the powerhouse. Subject to regional approval, this group would decide on general concerns of a municipal nature – where new houses and government installations would be placed, which roads needed upgrading, where streetlighting should be installed. Usual topics of general conversation were the problems of Eskimo drinking and social life or else the lack of ability of the regional offices to understand the reality of community life.

The Advisory Council was thus a small clique of the traditional colonial powers in the community. All members saw themselves primarily responsible to agencies and interests outside of the community. When the territorial government began its Local Government Program in 1968-69, the common perception, both within communities and in the government, was that councils would now be elected. The elected settlement council was still to be advisory to the area administrator, later called the settlement manager, until it became a hamlet. The elected council would deal with the municipal services of the settlement, specifically water delivery, sewage and garbage pick-up, roads and airstrips, fire protection, and a continuation of the Community Development Fund, now called the Per Capita Grant.

Another major influence on the Settlement Council program was the previously introduced low-cost housing program. First introduced into the Eastern Arctic in 1964, the Housing Association Program was seen as a successful first step toward developing self-government. In conversations with the regional director of the Fort Smith Region in 1968-69, the Local Government Settlement Council Program was described as an evolution of the Housing Association Program to include local involvement in municipal services in the community. The major aspects of the Housing Association Program are instructive. The structure, responsibility, eligibility, and method of elections were strictly predefined. Housing associations were granted basically three areas of responsibility: responsibility to collect rent, responsibility to assign tenants, and responsibility to provide maintenance; each of these areas had strict guidelines. Housing associations had no say in the design of homes or in the number of houses assigned to a community; they had no power to modify or reform the system under which they operated.

Consequently, one of the effects of this program has been to reinforce a setting where a government official, usually white, is the 'expert' on how the community is to deal with its housing problems. The experience and understanding of community residents is inadequate as a basis for judgment because the rules and procedures are alien to the background of the residents. To operate successfully on a housing association one must look not to one's own cultural background but must adapt to a set of externally imposed rules and procedures. The program makes local residents dependent on government officials for expertise.

The development of the local government model

Although the territorial government presented municipal councils as an opportunity for communities to run their own affairs, it is interesting to examine some of the specifics by which this local autonomy was to evolve. The structure of the council was completely predetermined prior to its introduction into the communities.

It was the bureaucrats of the territorial administration, ultimately responsible to Ottawa, who designed the structures and delineated the powers of local councils. A passage from an article by Dave Flynn, one of the civil servants responsible for these decisions, is particularly revealing on this point:

The new Department of Local Government in 1967 decided to continue the system of democratic government already started in the North. This was done partly for continuity. The larger centres already were incorporated as municipalities; a few others were on their way toward control of their own affairs.

In addition, we, the territorial staff in charge of local government, had to remember the overall purpose of the Department of Local Government: to prepare for additional responsibility at the territorial level. We had to satisfy Ottawa that government at the local level was 'legitimate.' This meant it had to be *representative* and *responsible*, two key principles of democratic government.

Mr Flynn's comments accurately reflect the essential colonialism underlying the efforts of the territorial administration's approach to political development. First, Mr Flynn clearly shows that the overall purpose of the program was not the development of community level political autonomy *per se* but rather the satisfaction of conditions set by Ottawa which would lead to an increased transfer of responsibilities to the territorial administration. Local government in the communities was simply the means by which the territorial administration could justify gaining increased administrative responsibilities from Ottawa.

The second telling indication of colonialism is Mr Flynn's assumed right to design a system of government for the Dene and Inuit. Mr Flynn implies that the only system of local government in the North worth examining was that of the incorporated municipalities (in 1967, Fort Smith, Inuvik, Hay River, and Yellowknife). The idea that either the Dene or Inuit might already have a system of government appears to be ignored. To my knowledge, it was never considered that the peoples being governed might wish to have some say in the design of their own government. The territorial administration apparently saw no contradiction in talking of people governing their own affairs while at the same time imposing a completely predetermined and alien government structure for such decision-making.

Later in his article Mr Flynn disallows the possibility of the evolution of traditional Dene forms of government:

At first we were told that in Indian communities the traditional Chief represented the community. In the first place, we argued, the Chiefs were not usually traditional. They were chosen originally by the Department of Indian Affairs as a representative for certain purposes of the federal government, ranging from the signing of treaties to greeting V.I.P.'s. Secondly, the Chiefs were apparently no longer representatives of the Indian community judging by the number of delegations opposing the Chief's policies. Finally, Chiefs were in no way representative of non-Indian residents of the communities.

Clearly, the territorial administration was not prepared to consider chiefs and band councils as a form of local government for its purposes. Instead, the Department of Local Government took it upon itself to design in specific detail the form and structure which local government would take.

A complex suggested constitution was drawn up for the approval of settlement councils. A training manual was also designed for instruction in the use of this new form of decision-making. The manual explains how to deal with the members of the community who might attend meetings and wish to get involved in the decision-making.

8.1 *When members of the community or other visitors attend council meetings.*

Although the public has a right to attend council meetings, the public has no special right to take part in council discussions but the council, through the chairman, may, if it wishes, ask or invite any member of the public or special visitor to join the discussion. The Chairman must make sure that the visitor's remarks are to the point and as brief as possible. When the discussion has ended and before the vote is taken, the chairman should thank the visitor who then withdraws from the proceedings to the back of the room away from the council table.

If any member of the public interrupts or disturbs a council meeting in any way, he may be asked to leave and if he will not do so, the assistance of a police officer may be obtained in removing the offender. In the event of a great deal of disturbance, after repeated calls for order by the Chairman, the Chairman should adjourn the meeting stating his reasons for doing so and naming the date, time and place of the next meeting.

It is self-evident how these suggestions served to destroy and undermine traditional decision-making processes.

The local government model

The model chosen by the territorial administration was effectively a southern municipal council. The process and content of such a structure contradicts the more traditional decision-making patterns of the Dene. Instead of a consensus method, a parliamentary procedure of majority rule was chosen. Instead of community involvement, participation was actively discouraged in favour of a strict principle of representative leadership.

Early in the introduction of these councils, development officers encouraged the use of native languages on the council. It appears significant that such a move had to be encouraged by the development officers, and was by no means spontaneous. However, in settlements with which I am familiar, the use of the local language was abandoned. The reasons given by the local people were that there are no words for council rules; if you are going to speak in a native language, then you are going to have to use native rules.

The over-all nature of the settlement council can be seen to be based in southern culture. It is bound to a culture which has an elitist decision-making pattern and does not expect or encourage broad involvement of its citizenry. It assumes the need for quick, business-like decisions without allowing time for reaching consensus. The area of responsibilities of the council is based on an assumption of an evolving tax base suited to a culture which has an ethic of private property and ownership. The council, in effect, becomes the forum for working out the interests arising out of the ownership of private property. The range of responsibilities delegated to the council – roads, airstrips, street-lights, water, sewage, and garbage – are prime topics of community discussion only in a private propertied, tax-based culture. When each person owns his own property or business, then these are the matters which the individual interests must collectively work out. In cultures not based on an ethic of private ownership, such topics are incidental to other collective problems. With the Dene, some of the more central collective issues might be organizing community hunts, deterioration of trapping lands, education, and care of the elders. Yet, councils have been told that such matters are not their responsibility; rather, they are the responsibility of various government agencies involved.

Another rather curious feature of the settlement council model is the concept of 'responsibility' envisaged by the territorial administration. In his article, Mr Flynn outlines the responsibility of the settlement councils:

The second democratic principle we insisted upon was that of *responsibility*. This meant responsibility to those who elected the Council and to those who provided the funds for operating the community. In the South the people who elect a Council also pay taxes for that Council's budget and, therefore, the Council's prime responsibility is to the electorate. In most northern communities, on the other hand, little money is available for local budgets so that as a result Councils have a dual responsibility: to the local residents whom they represent and to the senior government which supplies their operating budget.

In my experience, responsibility was generally defined as indicated in Mr Flynn's article. The 'prime responsibility' of the councils was to whoever provided the funds. When communities became tax-based, their prime responsibility would then be to the taxpayers. Until that time, it was to the Northwest Territories administration.

It follows that the territorial administration viewed settlement councils as local administrative units. They were not viewed as political bodies in the sense that they would be bodies whose function was to represent the views, values, and interests of the electorate they represented. Rather, their function was seen as primarily administrative.

Settlement councils in the communities

The Department of Local Government was given a mandate to undertake the initiation of settlement councils into the communities. An education process was planned whereby settlement managers, responsible to the executive, would assist the fledgling local councils in their efforts to gain sophistication. Once a community turned hamlet, it was considered by definition to be developed. Municipalities such as towns, villages, or cities were considered to represent the ultimate evolution of the settlement council model.

According to the Annual Report of the Commissioner of the NWT for 1972: 'Throughout 1972 the Department of Local Government continued to assist in the transfer of governmental responsibilities to settlements. The success of this program is heavily dependent upon the willingness of communities to accept responsibilities.' (The Report listed pipeline development ahead of settlement councils as a concern of the Department of Local Government, which in itself speaks volumes.) To suggest that communities had a questionable willingness to accept responsibility hardly gets to the dynamics created by the Local Government Program. Certainly, the settlement councils were greeted with some confusion. On the one hand, people eagerly acknowledged that they wished to run their own affairs. There were repeated comments by community people to the effect that natives should be allowed to do that; the government or whites should not control native people. Therefore, the local government concept was welcomed.

On the other hand, the emphasis on parliamentary procedure, on sticking to the issues of garbage, sewage, and water confused and frustrated people to the point where they wondered what all this had to do with running their own affairs. Rumours of major developments were beginning, but councils were told that these were not their responsibility. The fact that councils could not act on decisions until they received government approval made it even more unclear as to what the government meant by 'accepting responsiblities.'

From my experience, I think now that almost without exception councils were perceived as foreign institutions whose purpose was, in the main, to serve interests outside the native community. I can recall various discussions in different communities where native people, often councillors, would maintain that their particular settlement or hamlet council was part of the territorial administration, not part of the community; and I would counterargue that the council was part of the community and that the community could use the council to express their own ideas and interests. The sense of alienation was pervasive, however.

Hugh Brody describes the contradictions inherent in the position of the administrator, indeed the whole government, vis-à-vis the local native population in Eskimo communities during this initial phase.

The administrators thus find themselves in a curious position. On the one hand, they urge the Eskimo community to believe that every effort is being made to give them responsibility for their own affairs. On the other hand, they insist that many of the affairs that the Eskimos regard as most important cannot be included within their sphere of responsibility. They soon realize that all fundamental decisions are still to be made by whites. It seems likely, therefore, that the Local Government Programs, in the context of the Eskimos' sense of subordinate status, have accelerated that withdrawal and indifference which the local government programs are specially aimed at preventing.

There was a hopeful belief on my part, and on the part of many other local government development officers, that communities would take over the settlement councils and ultimately reform them to use them for their own interests and purposes. On reflection, such a hope seems rather fanciful. Any serious attempts to use the council structure beyond its predefined municipal service function were soundly rebuffed.

Following from the 1966 recommendations of the Carrothers Commission (the Advisory Commission on the Development of Government in the Northwest Territories), there was initially a government policy of encouraging regional councils. The Carrothers Report recognized the importance of people becoming aware of themselves as collective units, with rights to organize on a collective basis. But it did not take long before it was recognized that such collective activity was particularly problematic for the administration. Such gatherings were politely tolerated at first. Soon a policy emerged that the Commissioner of the NWT would have to approve all details, including agenda and delegates, prior to the event. The responsible local government official also had to be included among the delegates. Generally such plans were perfunctorily approved. However, when Fort Good Hope, Fort Franklin, Fort Norman, Fort Wrigley, and Norman Wells decided to hold a regional conference in Fort Norman in the fall of 1973, approval was not so automatic. Fort Wrigley had taken a strong stand against the construction of the Mackenzie highway and the Administration feared that such an attitude might spread. Fort Norman, the organizing community, was therefore told that it would be inconvenient to hold a regional council at that time; it was implied that funding was short. The region persisted. The Director of Local Government advised me that the Minister had indicated that there was to be no regional gathering, especially not one involving Fort Wrigley. The councils, it was argued, should have some respect for the government. If the government felt that the present timing for a regional conference would be difficult, then council should realize that it would be in their best interest to wait until they had government approval. The government does not change quickly and councils must learn to be realistic about what they can expect from the government, it was stated.

The Local Government position towards band councils also remains the same. Although in Arctic Red River, the community decided that the band council structure should develop to include the municipal function of a settlement council, the Director of Local Government indicated that he would permit such a body as long as it was viewed as a 'pre-Settlement Council' which would be encouraged to adopt normal settlement council structure and procedure as soon as possible.

It is now my opinion that, despite official declarations to the contrary, and despite the individual beliefs of various local government officers, the territorial administration as a whole has had no serious intent of allowing either communities or native peoples any significant degree of autonomy or any real chance to run their own affairs. One may well ask why the territorial administration bothered with a Local Government Program at all if it did not intend to allow people greater political autonomy. Why did it put so much effort into establishing local councils?

The answer is quite simple. It was very much in the interest of the territorial administration to undertake such a program to maintain and enhance its own position. The major interests of the territorial administration were served in a number of ways. The administration wished to get a greater degree of administrative control from Ottawa. Ottawa set a condition to such a transfer, the condition being that the territorial administration had to develop a greater appearance of being a legitimate democratic government in the North. This appearance could be created through the establishment of a municipal government infrastructure, Ottawa stated. There was one important limitation on this municipal infrastructure, however, if the territorial administration wished to gain control from Ottawa. Chiefs and band councils, through the treaties and the Indian Act, were a direct federal responsibility. To acknowledge the chiefs and band councils as a legitimate form of local government would therefore defeat the territorial administration's purpose. Thus, the territorial administration could argue for a greater control over northern administration if it could develop a municipal infrastructure controlled through territorial ordinances; that is, an infrastructure which excluded chiefs and band councils. The territorial administration therefore adopted an ideology which didn't acknowledge race or cultural difference: 'We're all northerners.'

There is another way in which the interests of the territorial administration were served by the Local Government Program. At the time of transfer of federal to territorial administration in the North, there were many federal civil servants who chose not to become part of the territorial administration. There was, at that time, considerable talk and wishful thinking that the territorial administration was hopelessly ill-equipped to carry on and that undoubtedly the federal government would have to reassert itself within a short while. Thus, the territorial administration needed very quickly to establish credibility within the North. By including community residents and pretending to let people run their own affairs, the Local Government Program initially won the allegiance of many native northerners for the territorial government.

Development versus administration

In the January 1974 sitting of Territorial Council, a motion was passed which asked the Department of Local Government to involve the communities in preparing a philosophy paper which would outline the philosophy of the department. The community meetings subsequently held in Dene settlements produced a consistent response. The Dene did not view settlement or hamlet councils as their own community institutions. Settlement councils were seen as imposed, belonging to the government. Repeatedly, chiefs and band councils were seen as the true community government.

The philosophy paper reported this. It also warned of the situation within the larger municipalities. The territorial administration viewed towns, villages, and cities as a more highly evolved form of community government, but the point of view of the native people in such centres was rarely considered. In relation to the process of establishing municipal government, the paper states: 'In a part of Canada two-thirds populated by native peoples, a continuation of this process raises depressing prospects.' The paper suggested that settlement councils be viewed as a process of political development, rather than as the creation of administrative structures:

The Department assumes then that as a first priority the development of municipal government must be seen as a means by which the original people of the Northwest Territories may come to play a major role in all levels of government. In practice, this confirms the emphasis on the obligations to the communities for political and social education toward a working awareness of their particular interests rather than exclusively providing administrative institutions as the communities move through levels of incorporation.

The philosophy paper was never discussed in Territorial Council, and any hope that the Local Government Program might be changed is gone. Within the Department of Local Government there had been a growing division between the 'developmental' interests which hold that local government should be primarily the process of development of political awareness, and the 'administrative' interests which hold that local government should be primarily the development of administrative structures. The fate of the philosophy paper essentially ensured that, from that point on, local government was to restrict itself to developing local administrative competence in a southern municipal structure. Roads, airstrips, water, sewage, garbage, town-planning, and lands became the primary concern of the department. Those involved in the preparation of the philosophy paper have since resigned from the territorial public service.

A memo, recently published in the media, from the Commissioner of the NWT to the Director of Local Government, dated 12 December 1975, confirms that the struggle within the department to make local government anything other than the imposition of southern municipal structures, is now over. The Commissioner wrote: 'I intend to insist in the new year that Local Government concentrate on the *mechanics* of preparing communities for hamlet and village status.' The Commissioner goes on to quote from notes made by Mr Ewan Cotterill (the Assistant Commissioner of the NWT, now Assistant Deputy Minister of Northern Affairs in Ottawa) regarding the Local Government program:

The basic thrust of the Development Division since its inception has been that of creating political awareness at the settlement level in the Northwest Territories. This thrust is no longer valid in that a good level of political awareness has been achieved, and the thrust must be changed to look beyond this basic development stage ... The kind of support now required by settlement and municipal councils is not available from the Department of Local Government and not being provided by them. Support is needed for the 'post political awareness' stage and this type of support is basically technical in nature, not philosophical.

It is not clear what the term 'post political awareness' means, but in my opinion, it is not in the interest of the Dene to define the present situation as requiring administrative rather than political development. At the same time, the notion that an arm of the territorial government, as a colonialist institution, can increase political awareness among the Dene, or the colonized, is a contradiction in terms which appears to have escaped even the most well-intended of local government people.

Conclusion

An analysis of the territorial administration's policy on the development of local government is, on reflection, really quite simple. While the territorial administration had direct interests in the appearance of a grass-roots political development, whenever the process threatened to become more than appearance, immediate attempts were made to limit and control the process. Rather than welcoming this as the success of the Local Government Program, the territorial administration has attempted to diffuse and limit that development by channelling it into administrative complexities and bureaucratic lethargy. In my opinion, it is this continued response of attempting to control, diffuse, and undermine the political self-determination of the native people within the Territories which most clearly shows the continuing colonial nature of the territorial administration in the North.

The territorial administration has an interest in maintaining and enhancing its control over the Dene and their land. It seeks to impose a system of institutions and decisions foreign to the Dene, a system serving non-Dene interests. Not only does this system not serve the Dene people, but instead it divides them and undermines their ability to maintain their own cultural patterns. The territorial administration does not represent the interests of the Dene, and the growth of the territorial administration in no way represents a decolonization of the Dene.

Although I have focused on the programs of the Department of Local Government, the situation within other departments is similar. In fact, it is the Department of Local Government which is generally regarded as the 'decolonizing wing' of the territorial administration, with the other departments having a somewhat more directly colonial view. Further, the very nature of the responsibilities given, and more importantly not given, to the territorial administration confirm its colonial character. With non-renewable resource development being the most important issue in the Territories today, it is the federal government, not the territorial administration, which maintains full and direct control in this area. Thus both in the carrying out of its responsibilities, and in the range of responsibilities it holds, the territorial administration is a colonial institution.

REFERENCES

Bean, Wilf, *Colonial Political Institutions in the Communities of the Northwest Territories* (Indian Brotherhood of the NWT, mimeo, March 1976)
Brody, Hugh, *The People's Land: Eskimos and Whites in the Eastern Arctic* (London, 1975)
Flynn, D., 'A Paper on the Philosophy of the Department of Local Government' (tabled in Territorial Council, Yellowknife, 13 Jan. 1975)
Settlement Councils: Some Notes for Secretary-Managers [Training Manual] (Department of Local Government, NWT July 1971)
Report of the Advisory Commission on the Development of Government in the Northwest Territories [Carrothers Commission] (Ottawa, 1966)

The Schools

Steve Kakfwi
Bob Overvold

STEVE KAKFWI

We, the Dene of the NWT, demand recognition of ourselves as a unique people and our right to self-determination. This is the reason for our push to have a land settlement with the federal government.

The purpose of government education in the North since its beginning has been to assimilate the Dene into the southern way of life. We the Dene have never been given recognition of our right to educate our young. Measures taken in the last years, which may look like the Dene have some control over education in the communities, are simply tokenism. The situation remains the same. The bureaucrats of the territorial government control education in the North, deciding what is best for the Dene. This is, and will remain, unacceptable to the Dene. Our Declaration clearly shows our will to collectively control our own future!

The Dene allowed the government to educate their young when schools were first built in the North. The Dene believed the government could take care of their interests and that they knew what was best for them. Then a few years ago, people started to realize that something was wrong. There developed a gap between the young and the old. The elders had much difficulty in relating to the young. Many of the young lost the language, the values, and the views which they had learned from their elders. The elders realized that what was happening to their young in school was not exactly what they wanted. The government was literally stealing young people from their families. They saw that, if the situation remained unchanged, they as a people would be destroyed in a relatively short time.

Some of the young Dene today are assimilated. From early childhood they have been told how lucky they were to be educated, to be intelligent enough to be educated, and how someday they too could be just like the whiteman, happy and rich with a big house. Many of the communities got a one-sided picture of southern society, for only the successful and the competent middle-class people came into the land of the Dene. They were all a picture of success and happiness. None of the failures or victims of the system came up to show us what we might become if we did not make it.

Today, there are many young Dene who have to face the reality of those who have not made it in the system. They are often alone, apart from their elders and rejected by the whites. They face a choice: continue to allow others to control their lives and their future and try to make it on non-Dene terms, or take action to ensure that they become with their people the ones to decide their own future. Together the Dene have decided to regain control of their own lives and their own future.

The Dene believe in sharing, in helping one another. The Dene believe in respect for the elders and in keeping close to them, for they are our educators, our guarantee that we can continue the Dene Nation long after they have gone.

How can we tolerate an educational system which is set up to fit into a capitalist world? Where the whole purpose in life is to become rich? Where the competitive spirit, the individualistic spirit, is far more important than the spirit of co-operation and the spirit of community? Where there is no room for mercy for the many who cannot make it? Where either you fit into the system or you are an outcast, a drop-out, a hippie? There are many labels for failures.

All people have a desire for continuity of themselves in the future. That is why people have families, so they can pass on to their children their values and their own way of relating to the world, so their children can continue as they had before them. No human being would allow anyone to suggest that they are worthless, that they have no right to insist on continuity of themselves in the future, no values worth passing on to others for the future. No people would knowingly give away their right to educate their children to someone else of whom they have no understanding, except where people have been led to believe they do not have such rights.

In many communities today, the schools operate more in the interests of transients and civil servants than of the Dene of the communities. The civil servants and many others are up here to provide services and to 'help' the Dene, but in coming into Dene communities they often are more harmful to the interests of the Dene.

It is their attitude and beliefs that are most harmful. For instance, a civil servant may move with his family into a small community for two or three years and demand that his children be taught in the standards of southern Canada. This argument comes up at meetings to discuss the possibilities of teaching native languages in the schools. Southern folks feel cheated if too much time is given to these 'special classes,' which they do not feel to be in their interests and do not want their children to attend. They would prefer to see their children and those of the Dene spend their time in an essentially southern education system, rather than recognizing the need of the Dene to build up their own understanding and pride of their own people, their own community, their own society.

The set-up of many small communities reflect the great differences between the white population and the Dene. Generally the white population are apart from the Dene; in fact, there is an attempt to create a situation in the community for them to live as much in the southern style as possible.

The school year is set up to suit the needs of the teachers and other civil servants; the summer is the best time to go for holidays, to go south for further education. There is really nothing in this set-up to reflect the needs of the Dene. Maybe if the government wasn't so bent on attracting this type of person up here, we would get more people that are willing to 'fit in' and attempt to understand the situation, rather than those that come up as self-appointed saviours and guardians of the Dene. It is for this type of people that the education in the North today reflects more the needs of southern society than of the Dene.

If other people feel threatened by the Dene demanding the right to control their own education then they should feel free to talk with us. They should not leave their affairs and concerns to be taken care of for them by the government, for that only breeds further mistrust and fear. The Dene ask that if people want to come up to live in the land of the Dene, they should realize they have stepped into our home and not just an extension of theirs in the south. If they do not like it here, then they can always go back south. Why should we make it easy for everyone to come and live amongst us, taking away more and more from us? Are we expected to become extinct as a people and be remembered as a people who lost everything they valued, including their children?

The educational system conditions you to think in ways which would best serve the system. One way people get 'brain-washed' is to believe that 'control' can only be obtained *through* the system and that one can only hope to get so much control and no more.

We are not allowed to question 'authority.' A few years ago the government announced plans to build the Mackenzie highway. The Dene along the Mackenzie opposed the highway. The government later came back with a solution: the 'Hire North Project.' This project sought out *individually* all the young, unemployed people of the communities and hired them to clear the right of way for the Mackenzie highway. Many of us actually believed this was something really helpful, when the whole idea was to buy out our resistance as a people. The young people, desperate for work, grabbed at the offer without any thought about the long-term effects of their actions. I saw it as a deliberate plot on the governments part to undermine the Dene's opposition to the highway, by dealing with us as individuals rather than collectively.

It is my belief that the Dene are unique, different from the people in other parts of Canada; that education in the North should reflect this uniqueness; that our own uniqueness must be built on the traditional values of the Dene along with the ideas and views we now have from our experience as a colonized people.

In a colonial system, one is not free to make choices. How you think and how you act is predetermined to a large extent by a higher authority. You are led to believe that the interests of this higher authority are the same as yours. Any process which keeps control in the hands of the territorial bureaucrats is colonial.

The pipeline is an example of how the system tries to tell people that its interests are the same as theirs. The Dene know that if the pipeline is built before a settlement of the land claim, it would only reinforce and enlarge the present colonial system.

The Dene wish to decolonize, so education should aim for that goal. By reflecting on our experience as a colonized people, we can strive to understand what it really means to be free, to be able to decide one's own future.

BOB OVERVOLD

I would like to express my opinion on how further development and perpetuation of the present education system in the NWT would, like any other major development, prejudice the Dene position of achieving a fair and just land claim settlement. At the same time I will argue the case of our right to develop an alternative education system – one based on local control and parental responsibility.

Many Dene are seriously questioning the present system of education and consequently are insisting on their right to initiate and develop an alternative educational system that will best meet their needs. The principles of an alternative system are to be defined in our land claims proposal. The premise of our proposal is our right to control all that happens on Dene land. This means controlling any type of development that we choose to pursue, be it political, economic, social, educational, etc. Thus to me it makes sense that the continuation and the further development of the present educational system would only jeopardize and greatly impede any effort of the Dene in initiating and developing an alternative education system.

The education system in the NWT over the past twenty to thirty years serves as a good example for the Dene of why not to adopt foreign systems in any area. Education over this period was and still is a system imposed on the Dene. Some of its characteristics are: a conditioning of people to respect an authority other than oneself; a conditioning of people to conform and not to question, to minimize one's own ability to make decisions based on one's own understanding of the world, and to become dependent instead on some external authority. The many areas of the failures of this system imposed on the Dene are well-documented, notably the high drop-out rate. The lesson to be learned from this experience is that no imposed educational system, no matter how well-intentioned, will work for the Dene. Instead, only one that is initiated and developed by the Dene and that is rooted in Dene tradition, culture, and values will be successful. Such a system would be based upon a person's environment and then expanded to provide knowledge of the culture or society that surrounds him. From a secure base that provides an understanding of one's self, a person can then choose what he/she wishes to know.

The importance of the Dene developing such an educational system is, to me, quite self-evident. If one accepts my evaluation of the present system in the NWT as being essentially no different from any other system in southern Canada, then I see the essence of that system for the average white child being that, when a child enters this formal system at the age of five or six, the system takes up without any break, reinforces, and builds upon all that the child has previously learned in his home and community. For the Dene child entering this system the case is the complete opposite. The same system means a severe break with his culture and starts him off at a disadvantage from which he most often never recovers. When an education policy is developed by the Dene in which content, philosophy, and methodology is not essentially foreign to them, as is now the case, then and only then will we stand a chance of succeeding. At least, it would mean that Dene children would enjoy the same democratic rights as other Canadians.

The present educational system up here is essentially no different from any other system to be found in southern Canada. Having gone through such a system, I have concluded that the primary affect of this education is to condition people so that they will be willing to serve the purposes of others. The primary effect of what I would consider to be true education would be to enable a person to better achieve personal freedom, to better understand and cope with what's happening around one's self. Such an awareness would lead to acting on one's own interest. True education can only mean to become aware that one makes choices and that one is responsible for those choices. In this manner, education is a process toward personal freedom and self-determination, not a process of control and de-humanization.

I'd like to describe briefly my experience of the education system in the NWT. Having gone through practically all levels of formal schooling - elementary, junior high, senior high, and post-secondary - I suppose I would be classified as the product of what the system of the past 20 years turned out. I don't know how pleased my parents are with the 'product,' but certainly I don't like it. By having 'successfully' (I use the word with tongue in cheek) gone through the system I have become almost totally conditioned to fit into southern society. On the other hand, what these many years have taken away from me has caused irrevocable damage to me as a Dene: it has caused a split between my parents and myself that may never be healed; it has caused me to lose my Dene language; and, most significantly, it has left me in somewhat of a limbo - not quite fitting into Dene society and not quite fitting into white society. These are just some of the many by-products of the system. God knows I would not wish them on anyone.

I spent eight years in residential schools: two years in one in Aklavik run by the Anglican Church, two years in one run by the Roman Catholic Church, and four years in one run by the federal government. I could go on for hours relating the negative aspects of having to live and get educated in such places, but I will limit myself to two points. First, traditionally Dene children learned from their parents. In residential schools the adult-child relationship was almost non-existent; most, if not all the school and residential staff were non-Dene and thus quite alien to the majority of Dene students. Second, because of the style of these institutions, their size, and layout, this meant that many rules and regulations had to be imposed and thus the students were essentially forced to conform.

This phenomenon of the whites being the 'educators' leads me to the point of how Dene were conditioned to think of what education is. Many Dene used to think, and many still do, of education as something white people do to us. It was common for the first graduates of the NWT Teacher Education program to relate stories of our first experience upon returning to Dene communities as teachers: it was normal to have Dene children and parents express total astonishment and disbelief of our being teachers.

My understanding of why the government wanted me to be a teacher is this: 'You were one of the few who were able to fit in and make it. Being Dene, you will thus be more successful in conditioning other Dene children to do likewise.'

It has taken me a long time, about twenty years, finally to start understanding what education really is. I feel that I am once again in 'kindergarten'
and that I face another twenty years of being educated; an education that will
de-condition me and allow me to achieve what I consider to be true education.

Aboriginal Rights

C. Gerald Sutton

Following the discovery of oil and gas in Prudhoe Bay, Alaska, in 1968, plans were initiated to construct a gas pipeline from Prudhoe Bay across to the Mackenzie Delta and then up the Mackenzie River valley to markets in the south. Application for a pipeline right of way was submitted in 1974 to the Government of Canada and an application made to the National Energy Board to construct a pipeline. The initial applicant was Canadian Arctic Gas (CAGPL) later to be followed by Foothills Pipe Lines Limited. The lands affected by these plans included lands in the Northwest Territories which since time immemorial have been the homelands of the aboriginal people, principally the Dene, although the Inuit also occupy lands in the Mackenzie Delta and Yukon coast. Mr Justice Thomas Berger was appointed as Commissioner to inquire into, and make recommendations on, the application for the right of way.

The traditional lands of the Dene have been and are subject to litigation. In 1973 the chiefs of the bands attempted to file a caveat in the Land Titles Office in Yellowknife, claiming ownership of their traditional lands by virtue of aboriginal rights. A caveat is a 'notice of claim' of an interest in certain lands. In the usual case, upon submission of the caveat to the Land Titles Office for filing, a notation of the caveat is made upon the title to the lands in question and anyone wishing to purchase those lands does so at his peril. The caveat is a warning of a claim of prior interest. With minor exceptions, the traditional lands of the Dene are not the subject of a title which has been registered in the land titles office, so at issue - apart from the claim of aboriginal rights - was the question of whether a caveat could be accepted in such a case.

In October 1973, Mr Justice William G. Morrow of the Supreme Court of the Northwest Territories ruled that the caveators - the chiefs - had sufficiently established a case for claiming aboriginal rights so as to warrant the filing of a caveat, and that further the caveat could be filed against lands which were not the subject of a title. This judgment was appealed by the

Crown to the Court of Appeals of the Northwest Territories and over-ruled
on the latter point only. The matter is now (fall 1976) under appeal to the
Supreme Court of Canada.

The Dene have asserted a claim to aboriginal rights and they argue – as
they have since 1971 – that if developments such as dams, parks, and pipelines are to be built this can only happen following a settlement with them on
the basis of their aboriginal rights. With respect to the pipeline, this position
has been captured in the slogan 'No pipeline before a land settlement.'

The meaning of aboriginal rights

Clearly, there is in Canadian law judicial recognition of something described
as aboriginal rights. While the content and meaning of those rights is unclear,
it is safe to say that they are a property right in the lands which native people
have traditionally used and occupied. But it is also safe to say that the native
people's perception of their aboriginal rights bears scant resemblance to this
judicial perception. To understand why this is so, that is, why this branch of
the law is so undeveloped, it is essential to review the history of aboriginal
rights.

According to English legal theory, new territory was acquired by one of
three principal methods: the occupation of previously unoccupied territory,
conquest, or cession. In other words, it was in these ways that English sovereignty was asserted over new territory or a transfer of sovereignty was affected. Thus, by the Treaty of Waitangi of 1840 the Maori of New Zealand
ceded sovereignty to the English Crown. For reasons that are not altogether
clear, it was not perceived by the English as essential that similar treaties be
made with the aboriginal people of North America. The treaties with the
Indian people of this continent are not treaties of cession of sovereignty but
treaties ceding rights to land in the sense of property rights only.

As judicial interpretation[1] would have it, English sovereignty was established through discovery followed by occupation and settlement. In the
demonstrable absence of conquest or cession, it was thus necessary to find
that either the territory was unoccupied, or in the words of the Judicial Committee of the Privy Council occupied by inhabitants 'so low in the scale of
social organization that their usages and conceptions are not to be reconciled
with the institutions or the legal ideas of civilized society.'[2] Clearly it was expedient that the aboriginal people be regarded as less than the European. It
served the logic of colonialism.

From the earliest times the assistance and generosity of the Indian people
was welcomed and relied upon by Europeans coming to North America; the
help of the Indian was essential to survival through the first winters.[3] But

once they were no longer needed, they were forgotten or their status in the eye of the European was diminished proportionately. Once their traditional lands became coveted, it appeared socially and legally necessary to see them as 'so low in the scale of social organization' that they were incapable of asserting that legal personality as nations or peoples asserted with such facility by Europeans.

This ethnocentrism of English colonial policy is reflected in judicial interpretation and unfortunately, in recent decisions of Canadian courts. In 1929 a Canadian judge declared:

But the Indians were never regarded as an independent power. A civilized nation first discovering a country of uncivilized people or savages held such country as its own until such time as by treaty it was transferred to some other civilized nation. The savages' rights of sovereignty even of ownership were never recognized.[4]

The quotation illustrates the confusion of sovereignty and property rights. This judge was wrong in ruling that even the ownership of traditional lands was not recognized in Canada.

As recently as 1970 a Canadian judge could argue:

The Indians of the mainland of British Columbia ... were undoubtedly a very primitive people with few of the institutions of civilized society, and none at all of our notions of private property ... I see no evidence to justify a conclusion that the aboriginal rights claimed by the successors of these primitive people are of a kind that it should be assumed that the Crown recognized them when it acquired the mainland of British Columbia by occupation.[5]

The Supreme Court of Canada fortunately did not adopt this line of reasoning, and Mr Justice Hall of that Court recognized that the law of aboriginal rights developed as part of a tradition based on 'ancient concepts formulated when understanding of the customs and culture of our original people was rudimentary and incomplete and when they were thought to be wholly without cohesion, laws or culture, in effect a subhuman species.'[6]

The aboriginal people of North America, then, were denied, in the eyes of the European colonizers, the status of sovereign peoples. The English did not, however, go so far as to deny them recognition of certain property rights to their traditional lands. This recognition of aboriginal ownership of their traditional lands is spelled out in the 'Magna Carta' of aboriginal rights, the Royal Proclamation of 1763. The Proclamation is a constitutional document establishing the government for the territory acquired by England from France following the Treaty of Paris. But it is also important in announcing a new policy relating to the Indians and their lands.

The Indians were to be protected in their use and occupation of their traditional hunting grounds. It was unlawful for anyone to purchase directly or to settle Indian lands. Only the Crown could purchase these lands, and the procedure for Crown acquisition was spelled out. From this follows the long tradition of acquisition of Indian lands by land cession treaty. The last of these treaties was Treaty 11 in the Northwest Territories in 1921.

There is some controversy as to whether the Royal Proclamation applies in the territorial sense to the present Northwest Territories, but the argument is academic as the courts have held that the recognition of aboriginal rights and the procedure to be followed in dealing with those rights as spelled out in the Royal Proclamation were matters of general English colonial policy and as such applied whether the Royal Proclamation applied or not. Moreover, there is in the Northwest Territories perhaps the clearest recognition in Canada of aboriginal rights. Upon the transfer of the Northwest Territories from England to Canada, the 'claims of the Indian tribes to compensation for lands required for purposes of settlement will be considered and settled in conformity with the equitable principles which have uniformly governed the British Crown in its dealings with the aborigines.'[7] Most significantly, this obligation of the government of Canada to settle with the Indians is constitutional by virtue of section 146 of the British North America Act, which specifies that the provisions of any order in council transferring the Northwest Territories shall have the same effect as if they were enacted by the Parliament of Great Britain. Other recognition of the right and policy is found in Treaties 8 and 11, of 1899 and 1921 respectively, which purport to extinguish aboriginal title to the traditional lands of the Dene in the Northwest Territories. (Title to be extinguished must first be recognized.) The early Dominion Lands Acts of 1872 through to 1908 recognized that 'the settlement of agricultural lands, or the lease of timber lands, or the purchase and sale of mineral lands' could not happen on lands 'the Indian title [to which] shall not at the time have been extinguished.'

There is, then, in Canadian law, judicial recognition of an aboriginal right; that right was seen to be a property right, a communal property right, and inalienable except to the Crown. The origins of this branch of the law are in the policies and practices developed by the English in the colonization and acquisition of North America.

The recognition of aboriginal rights and introduction of a new Indian policy in the Royal Proclamation of 1763 were based not on principles of decency and justice but colonial pragmatism. The encroachment of European settlers upon traditional lands and the frauds and abuses committed against the Indians were the cause of unrest, and it was perceived by the Crown that in the interest of keeping the peace it was necessary to pacify the Indians through confirmation of rights to traditional lands and centralization of 'Indian Affairs' so as to eliminate certain practices on the part of Europeans and the local governments.

Theoretically, the Indians were to be secured in the unmolested use and enjoyment of their lands and encroachment onto those lands by Europeans could only follow a purchase of those lands from the Indians by the Crown and then a purchase from the Crown. Thus, while no pressure existed to settle those lands, the Indians were secure. But once those lands were coveted for settlement, or developments such as railways, the recognition of the aboriginal title was made by the Crown so that it could be extinguished in order to open the way for settlement. The aboriginal right recognized in British colonial practice was therefore a very shallow one. The reality was that it was never intended that the right would afford any protection when it was needed most – when the pressure was on. The sordid history of this country is that aboriginal title was only recognized for the purpose of extinguishment, and then only when it was necessary to do so; and most of the Indian title was extinguished by treaty of cession at a time when the Indians were at their weakest and without a position of strength from which to bargain; the treaties covering the huge land mass of the prairies were made when the Indians were diseased, starving, and desperate.

Because the Indian title rights were effectively recognized only for the purpose of extinguishment, there is little law on the content of those rights. It is only in very recent times that those with an interest to pursue the question – the Indian people themselves – have been in a position to do so. Apart from lacking the knowledge of the system and the resources to pursue claims politically or through the courts, the organizing and raising of money for the pursuit of aboriginal rights were, for the period from 1927 to 1951, illegal by provisions in the Indian Act.

In fact, however, there is nothing in our law which *requires* that aboriginal rights be extinguished. It is revealing that in other jurisdictions it has not been found necessary to extinguish aboriginal title as has been the rule in North America. Examples are New Zealand, Fiji, and Papua New Guinea. Rather than extinguish aboriginal title and then leave the aboriginal peoples with 'reserves,' in those cases the aboriginal title to specific lands is converted to a form of title which is recognizable under the colonial legal system, and thus, theoretically at least, the aboriginal peoples are secured through the protection of the legal system of the dominant society.

The aboriginal peoples of Canada were powerless at those times in history when 'settlements' were made with them, and if they had not been powerless, the form of settlement might have been much different; they might well have insisted upon conversion of their title to one compatible with the English legal system. Certainly, they could have made a better bargain, even if extinguishment of their title was what was wanted.

Certain basic and harsh realities face anyone attempting a true understanding of the place of 'native rights' in Canadian law and society. European sovereignty was simply unilaterally imposed over North America. If it had happened pursuant to treaty or agreement, then much of what is so tragic in our history might have been avoided. It was that initial denial of sovereignty that denied to the Indian the right and opportunity to negotiate his place in Canadian society.

In the absence of a negotiated relationship between peoples, how can the relationship be other than exploitative? The double tragedy is that it would appear that the treaties were in the eyes of the Indians at the time precisely this negotiated relationship, though it is equally clear that the officials responsible and the government of Canada never intended that they be, in spite of the fact that they probably realized what the treaties meant to the Indians. The swindle lay not so much in 'beads and blankets' but, rather, in the cynical exploitation of solemn occasions and the pretence of negotiation between peoples. Canadian society is culpable and incomplete so long as this denial of the Indians as a people stands.

European sovereignty having been established, the property right of the aboriginal peoples was recognized by the European colonizer to the extent, and only to the extent, that it was necessary for him to do so. The result was the imposition of a dominant legal system - a European legal system - upon all the inhabitants of the continent, including those inhabitants who had since time immemorial used and occupied the land. These latter inhabitants were, of course, non-European, and the property relations of these aboriginal peoples were by definition quite different from the European.

While English law recognized the basic right of people to the use and enjoyment of their traditional lands, without the conversion of that title to a form permitting the protection of the English legal system, the aboriginal peoples remained helpless and dependent on the goodwill and morality of the colonial or dominant society. The right to unmolested use and enjoyment of traditional lands was only as good as the word, will, and integrity of colonial society.

In some jurisdictions, such as most of British Columbia and the Yukon, not even the minimum standards of law or morality were adhered to; title was not even recognized to the point that it was regarded necessary to extinguish it by treaty. In other jurisdictions, such as on the prairies, it was recognized that the Indian people had an aboriginal title to the lands they had used since time immemorial, and that it was necessary to extinguish that title before the land could become available for European use. This conformed to the minimum standards of decency, though in the end the bargain struck and the subsequent exploitation of once-powerful peoples are a tragic indictment of European appropriation of North America.

The same adherence to these minimum standards was followed in the Northwest Territories. Probably because this occurred at the end of the process of making treaties, it was done, however, in a way which did not satisfy even the process designed for other places and other times. The record preserved in the 'caveat case' and the exhaustive study of Father Fumoleau[8] shows that it was at best a pathetic attempt to extinguish Indian title.

Treaty 8 was made in 1899 in Northern Alberta, BC, Saskatchewan, and the southern extremities of the present Northwest Territories because it was considered legally essential and expedient to do so. The pressure came from the Klondike gold rush. Tension was growing amongst the Indians because of the invasion of insensitive miners and prospectors on their way to the Yukon, and it was considered expedient to treat with the Indians so as to mollify their fears and concerns. Moreover, it was long known that the region was a vast storehouse of minerals and oil. Particularly the Treaty was expanded into the Great Slave Lake area in 1900 because of known deposits of minerals, and it was considered legally essential to extinguish Indian title if these resources were to be exploited. Likewise for Treaty 11 in 1921, covering the Mackenzie Valley as far north as the Mackenzie Delta: the discovery of oil at Norman Wells made it essential in the opinion of the government that Indian title be extinguished.

But the manner in which this was done bore scant fidelity to the requirements envisaged by the Royal Proclamation. The government and treaty parties were driven by a desire to get it over with as soon as possible, and the evidence of eye-witnesses, including signatories and an interpreter, is to the effect that there was no agreement on the part of the Dene to surrender their rights to their land. Emphatically, they rejected the notion of reserves. There was thus not even the pretence of a negotiated agreement on the hollow issue of surrendered property rights. Nor was there the coercion of an agreement negotiated under perceived weakness, resignation, and great pressure as happened on the prairies. In the minds of the Dene, the treaties were and are peace and friendship treaties – that is, negotiated treaties or agreements between peoples, not land cession agreements.

Notwithstanding the tragic history that lies behind the development of this branch of the law, and whatever its inadequacies, the principle remains: that title to lands traditionally used and occupied was recognized as vested in the aboriginal peoples and access to those lands for non-aboriginal use was only to be made following a settlement with those peoples.

The recent settlements in Alaska and James Bay are based on this tradition of settling with aboriginal peoples, although in the case of James Bay negotiations took place while development proceeded. Aboriginal rights were extinguished in exchange for compensation in the way of money and some land in forms recognizable at Canadian law. In spite of the elaborate corporate networks and other 'innovations,' these settlements are not very new in form.

The form of the settlement is, of course, itself a matter for negotiation, and depending on the bargaining power of the aboriginal people a fair bargain could be struck. The sufficiency of the bargain will be reflected not only in the numbers involved (dollars and square miles of land) but the form as well. Legally, there is nothing that compels that the tradition of extinguishment be followed. It is only political expediency which binds us to that tradition. The sufficiency of the bargain will also depend on whether the representatives of the dominant society will be bound by basic moral principles, and whether the aboriginal peoples are now seen to have legal rights which were not recognized in darker times in the history of Canadian society.

A modern perspective on aboriginal rights

Assuming that our understanding of aboriginal customs and culture has changed in a progressive way, are there legal principles hitherto unrecognized which alter our perception of land settlement? Specifically, is it arguable that aboriginal rights includes more than simple property rights, and that therefore it is not only unjust and absurd, but illegal, to speak of extinguishment of those rights? Certainly, it would be most unfortunate for the integrity of Canadian society, and tragic for the struggle of aboriginal peoples, if the resolution of aboriginal land issues is to be fixed by legal perceptions and traditions developed at a time when the original people of this continent were regarded as 'in effect a subhuman species.'

Factually, there have been changes. These changes are dramatically illustrated from a review of the history of the Indian Act. Reserves are no longer, in effect, concentration camps. Indians are no longer legally prohibited from practising their culture and, most significantly, Indians since the late 1950s have been enfranchised, though this serves to remind us how recent the public and official perception of Indians has changed.

This may not be occasion to celebrate, but it does reveal that times have changed. Has the law changed, or is it capable of changing? Significantly, the enfranchisement of the Indian people suggests that the Indian people are now perceived as capable of the responsible exercise of the franchise. Does it not follow that they are likewise capable of running their affairs in ways that do not require the extinguishment of their rights and their restriction to sanctuaries where they will be looked after and protected as wards of the state until such time as they become extinct or 'worthy' of assimilation?

Yet more significantly, the global view of the rights of non-Europeans has altered dramatically in recent decades. European empires have collapsed and scores of nation states of non-European peoples have been born. Together with this has occurred exciting developments in mankind's perceptions of human rights. Standards have been set forth in international instruments, beginning with the Universal Declaration of Human Rights adopted by the General Assembly of the United Nations in 1948, which are regarded by a substantial sector of the world community as compelling. Many of these standards have evolved beyond mere moral precepts and have assumed the status of principles of public international law or the customary law of nations.

The development of principles and rights often described as human rights, and the further evolution of these into principles and rights of public international law, has happened in such a way that people do not seem automatically to associate such rights and principles with the aboriginal peoples of North America. There is, of course, no reason why the association should not be made; and perhaps with more general recognition of the 'Fourth World' of the aboriginal minorities within countries, the association will be made.

It is argued that the following principles, which bear upon the question of whether the rights of the Dene are more than extinguishable property rights, are principles of public international law, that is, they are legal and not only moral precepts.

1 The Dene as a distinct people are an 'ethnic and linguistic' minority within the meaning of Article 27 of the International Covenant on Civil and Political Rights[9] and have the right to the 'enjoyment of their culture.' While Canada is not a signatory to the Covenant (ostensibly because of the problems created by the division of powers between the federal government and the provinces) and is therefore not bound in terms of international treaty obligations, the principle set forth in the covenant constitutes general international law and thus binds Canada.

2 Since 1945, the right to self-determination has come to be recognized as a legal precept and not merely a political desideratum. The key development was the reference to the 'principle of equal rights and self-determination of peoples' in Article 1(2), Article 55, and Articles 73-74 of the Charter of the United Nations. The principle has been confirmed by the practice of the member states expressed through the organs of the United Nations, resolu-

tions of the General Assembly, and subsequent instruments such as the International Covenant on Civil and Political Rights and the International Covenant on Economic, Social and Cultural Rights.

ILO Convention no. 107, 'Concerning the Protection and Integration of Indigenous and other Tribal and Semi-Tribal Populations in Independent Countries,' a convention of the General Conference of the International Labour Organization of June 26, 1957, contains specific reference to native peoples amongst whom should be classed the Dene. The Convention recognizes 'the right of ownership, collective or individual of the members of the population concerned, over the lands which those populations traditionally occupy ...' and respects the 'procedures for the transmission of rights of ownership and use of land which are established by the customs of the populations concerned ...' While Canada is not a signatory to the Convention,[10] it is the best evidence of international standards in respect of the protection of traditional cultures.

Thus, it can be said with conviction that indeed times have changed and, in particular, the law has changed. It no longer makes sense to speak of extinguishment of rights as though all that were included were mere property rights. The Dene as aboriginal peoples have significant, internationally recognized political or human rights, including the right to enjoyment of culture and the right to self-determination. In other words, the Dene *as a people* have a right to survival and self-development. To speak of extinguishment of rights in this context is ludicrous.

Clearly, therefore, in applying the principle developed in English and Canadian law that settlers and developers might only proceed following a land settlement with the aboriginal peoples in occupation of their traditional lands, projects such as the proposed pipeline cannot lawfully proceed without a settlement with the Dene which recognizes not only their property rights but their political and human rights as well.

The real context of the pipeline proposal

The Northwest Territories is a colony. Control is exercised out of Ottawa through the bureaucracies of both the federal and territorial governments. The Territorial Council is effectively powerless and it and the municipal councils introduced by the territorial administration have proven to be alien and ineffective institutions to the Dene. The Dene and Inuit are a majority in the Northwest Territories, and together they retain a slim majority advantage in the population of the Mackenzie Valley. The non-native population is almost exclusively transient, many of them bureaucrats, and concentrated in larger settlements.

Although the Dene have suffered much destruction from their colonial experience, their life-style is not significantly different from the traditional. They have survived as a distinct people with a unique culture and use the resources of their traditional lands in ways not dissimilar to their ancestors. In this sense, the Dene have not suffered the decimation experienced by their cousins in southern Canada. Given the relatively undeveloped state of the polity and economy of the Northwest Territories, the opportunity exists for a radical departure from the traditions of destruction and exploitation that occurred in the colonization of Indian land in the rest of Canada.

The proposed Mackenzie Valley pipeline must be seen in this broad perspective. It has been described as the largest developmental project in the history of the country and is frequently compared to the construction of the CPR. In fact, the latter project was significant both from the perspective of the political development of western Canada and the fortunes of the Indian people. The West was changed forever and the Indians suffered almost indescribable destruction.

Such developments assume overwhelming significance because they are much more than the development itself. Such developments are the vanguard of the 'conquest of the last frontiers' and invariably the aboriginal people suffer. Without adequate protection for the role of the aboriginal people in the radically changed society resulting from such developments, their destruction is inevitable. The evolution of adequate political institutions is essential, or history repeats itself.

The question of land settlement thus assumes critical significance. It is, therefore, incorrect to focus solely on the development itself, as the developers would like us to do. The issue is: where does the development fit into the broader question of the evolution of institutions ensuring the self-determination of peoples and justice for all, and not *vice versa*. Thus, land settlement and not the pipeline is *the* issue, and it is specious logic to look at the pipeline as an isolated development.

Principles of public international law

While land settlement is *the* issue, that is not to say that there are not principles in international law which are relevant to the pipeline *per se*. Again, these principles are law and not merely standards of morality, though moral standards are surely themselves critical.

The proposed pipeline, like similar massive developments in frontier regions in the past, will invariably result in destruction to traditional, land-based aboriginal peoples. This destruction, apart from the disruption of the traditional economy through environmental degradation, occurs in the form of the disruption and dislocation of the community. The cultural nervous system is disrupted, control over the life and future of the community is lost, and the consequences are tragic. There occur loss of language and traditions, alcoholism, self-destruction, and so on.

Given the above, it can be asserted that the construction of the proposed pipeline will be in violation of the two previously stated principles of public international law:

1 The pipeline project would be an infringement of the right of the Dene 'to enjoy their own culture' as enshrined in the International Covenant on Civil and Political Rights.

2 The extensive displacement and destabilization of the Dene community would be akin to the cruder process of deportation of ethnic groups from their homelands, a process which is a particularly clear example of the denial of the right to self-determination.

In addition, the proposed pipeline would be in violation of yet another principle of international law:

3 The extensive displacement and destabilization of the Dene community would amount to a violation of the broadly recognized principle of the right of racial non-discrimination. The discrimination comes in the form of the inordinate burden placed upon the Dene. The majority of the population in the Mackenzie Valley are the Dene, who are a distinct ethnic group. Thus the Dene would bear almost exclusively the costs of a development, the benefits of which accrue elsewhere. And when the community concerned has a traditional way of life, and the consequences include irreversible cultural change and loss of control over the life and future of the community, the burden is even greater.

Furthermore, it is no excuse to say after the fact that the consequences were not intended. Recklessness is a basis of legal responsibility, and to proceed with knowledge of the risk is recklessness. Also, the principle of non-discrimination, or equality, requires not merely formal equality but effective equality, that is, equality in fact. Thus, it is no answer to say that the people who live in the vicinity of a major project suffer inevitable damage. Because the people in question are a distinct ethnic minority (within Canada) they have a right of equality with the majority; that equality must be effective equality if it is to mean anything at all. Finally, since benevolent or compensatory discrimination is not unlawful, measures designed to assist or maintain the rights of minorities are not unlawful.

Consequently, the advance of pipeline construction without a settlement which effectively protects and preserves the rights of the Dene would be a violation of the principle of racial non-discrimination and unlawful. But special measures, such as a land settlement to protect the rights of the Dene, are not unlawful.

On the basis of the foregoing, it is inconceivable to think of the granting of a right of way for a pipeline, or construction of a pipeline, without first developing and implementing a settlement with the aboriginal people of the Mackenzie Valley which will ensure the survival of the Dene as a people and the enjoyment of their human rights.

Expropriation

In states such as Canada, it is recognized within the legal system that the state has power to expropriate lands for public purposes subject to a right of compensation. Specifically, it is provided in the National Energy Board Act that lands can be expropriated for pipeline right of ways and the procedures for expropriation in the Railway Act are incorporated for that purpose. The theory is that the public interest pre-empts the right of the individual, and the assumption is that the individual is not harmed in any serious way. He is seen to be culturally and economically mobile, and with the compensation he receives he readily moves his place of residence. In the same way the individual is seen as a property owner and that which is expropriated is his property.

This, of course, takes no account of the interests of a community who are not so mobile in the above sense, and whose identity is territorially defined. Moreover, it makes no sense to conceive of such a group as mere property owners. The expropriation of lands is much more than the expropriation of property rights. Thus, it makes no more sense to speak of expropriation of rights than it does to speak of extinguishment of rights.

In addition to this, the notion of expropriation in advance of a land settlement is not compatible with the law of aboriginal rights developed over time in Canadian law. The rationale, expressed for example in the Royal Proclamation, is that the aboriginal people are to be protected and unmolested in the use and occupation of their lands until such time as a settlement is made. With the conversion of their property right to a form compatible with the European legal system – or the extinguishment of rights and vesting of 'new' or European forms of property rights such as reserves or freehold – then and only then does it make sense to speak of expropriation. And even then expropriation of Indian lands, such as reserves, becomes a special case and quite different from the norm.

Conclusion

The legal rights of aboriginal peoples have largely been a reflection of colonial policy in North America. Because colonization did not happen in enlightened

times, those rights fall far short of the standards expected and demanded by
Europeans for themselves. But recent decades have witnessed great changes in
the standards of morality relating to colonization and non-European peoples,
and it is argued in this paper that the legal rights of aboriginal peoples have
grown with these changes. Specifically, it is argued that aboriginal peoples
have certain basic rights, such as the all important right to self-determination,
which are now legal rights under public international law.

Whether those rights will, in fact, be recognized will depend on the ability
of the Dene to enforce their rights and the capacity of the government of
Canada and people of Canada to recognize that, indeed, times have changed.

NOTES

This paper draws upon the evidence of Mr Douglas Sanders on behalf of the Indian
Brotherhood of the NWT to the Berger Inquiry, and an opinion of Dr Ian Brownlie
of Oxford University on relevant principles of international law prepared for the
Brotherhood for use at the Berger Inquiry. It also relies upon an unpublished paper
by Mr Brian Slattery, 'The Land Rights of Indigenous Canadian Peoples: Interna-
tional Aspects' (Faculty of Law, University of Dar es Salaam, 1974) and an article by
Professor J.C. Smith of the University of British Columbia, 'The Concept of Native
Title' (1974) 24 *University of Toronto Law Journal.*

1 Leading decisions are those of Chief Justice Marshall of the United States Supreme
  Court: *Johnson v McIntosh* (1823) 8 Wheaton 543 and *Worcester v Georgia* (1832)
  6 Peters 512; and the leading case in Canadian law, the decision of the Judicial Committee of the Privy Council, *St. Catherines Milling v The Queen* (1888) 14 AC 46
2 *In Re Southern Rhodesia* (1919) AC 211
3 See George Manuel and Michael Posluns, *The Fourth World* (Don Mills, 1974)
4 *Rex v Syliboy* [1929] 1 DLR 307 at 313
5 *Calder et al. v Attorney-General* (1970) 13 DLR (3d) 64 at 66
6 *Calder et al. v Attorney-General* (1973) SCR 313
7 Schedule A to the Imperial Order in Council of 1870
8 René Fumoleau, *As Long As This Land Shall Last* (Toronto, 1975)
9 Following the adoption of the Universal Declaration of Rights in 1948, steps were
  taken to have the rights implemented in the form of international treaty rights. The
  rights were set out in two covenants, the International Covenant on Civil and Political Rights and the International Covenant on Economic, Social and Cultural Rights.
  These covenants were unanimously adopted by the General Assembly in 1966.
10 In sessions of the International Labour Conference when proposed texts for the convention were being considered, Canadian representatives argued that many of the
  principles in the Convention were already applied in Canada and it would be a retro-
  gressive step if the proposed instrument were applied to the indigenous people of
  Canada, who were seen as being at a more advanced stage of development than the
  indigenous people for whom the Convention was designed. The government of Canada was against an international instrument and preferred that the United Nations
  set up study groups.

The Dene Nation and Confederation

Peter H. Russell

This paper focuses on two related questions: (1) How does the concept of a Dene nation square with the principles of the Canadian constitution? (2) Should Canada respond to the Dene people's claim for recognition of their rights before or after the construction of a pipeline through their traditional homeland?

Let me begin with the first question. To answer it we must first examine the concept of the Dene nation and see what juridical and political arrangements are entailed by that concept. Second, we must set our understanding of the Dene nation alongside the letter and the spirit of the Canadian constitution in order to decide whether or not recognition of the Dene's basic claim to be regarded as a nation within Canada is consistent with the Canadian constitution.

For an understanding of the concept of the Dene nation, I rely primarily on the statement entitled the Dene Declaration. The central concept in this Declaration is that of 'nation.' We must first come to terms with that concept.

There are two ways in which the word 'nation' has been used. The oldest and most continuous usage associates the concept of nation or nationality with what is basically a cultural entity. The American historian, Carlton Hayes, thus defines a nationality as 'a group of people who speak either the same language or closely related dialects, who cherish common historical traditions, and who constitute or think they constitute a distinct cultural society.' Similarly, the European historian Georg Jellinek defines nation as 'a multitude of humans characterized by common and unique cultural factors. This multitude shares in a common historical past and is linked by an awareness of its uniqueness' (cited in Heiman). Nations and nationalities so defined existed in human history as social and cultural collectivities long before the emergence of the nation state and that other usage of nation and nationality which is primarily legal and juridical. It is the distinctive mark of the modern political era, beginning about the sixteenth century, to have organized the world into nation states, each governed by a sovereign authority based on a

distinct territory and claiming a monopoly of legal control over all who inhabit that territory and legal independence from any external authority. In
this context, nation is identified with the sovereign state: the nation is the
sovereign legal entity which participates as an individual and independent
member in the international community of nations, and nationality is a legal
capacity bestowed by the sovereign nation on all of its citizens regardless of
their cultural characteristics.

Now both usages of the words nation and nationality survive in the modern world, including contemporary Canada. Canada is clearly a nation in the
juridical or legal sense: it is an independent sovereign nation state. One of the
basic aims of the confederation movement which created Canada was to establish a new nation and a new nationality. But this new nationality was not to
entail a cultural uniformity. On the contrary, as George Etienne Cartier stated
in the Confederation Debates, 'Now, when we were united together, if union
were attained, we would form a political nationality, with which neither the
national origin, nor the religion of any individual would interfere.' He went
on to elaborate how the different nations (or 'races' as he called them) in the
cultural sense should survive within this new juridical nation: 'In our own
Federation we should have Catholic and Protestant, English, French, Irish and
Scottish, and each by his efforts and his success would increase the prosperity
and glory of the new Confederacy.' (Waite)

Thus, both usages of the word nation have survived in Canada. The first,
connoting an ethnic, cultural, or sociological entity has been most used in
French Canada. This usage has not been a separatist term. It has been used by
those who wish their distinctive national culture to survive within the Canadian nation. This double usage, as Eugene Forsey has pointed out 'can, theoretically, give rise to ambiguities and misunderstandings. But in practice,
surely the context makes it tolerably clear which of the two we mean.' Further, insisting on the continuation of the double usage, he asks, 'Are we really
free to choose one meaning of the word "nation" and "national" and discard
the other? I don't think we have any right to play ducks and drakes with dic-
tionary, English or French, in this fashion.'

Taking our cue from Senator Forsey, we can now return to the Dene
Declaration and see what is meant by 'nation' as used in that context. The
answer is clear. The concept of nation, the right to be recognized as a national
group, as used and claimed by the Dene people, is in accord with the first and
oldest usage of these terms. They are claiming the right to survive as a distinct
cultural entity 'within the country of Canada.'

The Dene's willingness to submit to the legal sovereignty of the Canadian
nation state, while clear enough, is given somewhat grudgingly as a submission

to a hard fact of life – to *real politik*. This is not surprising. Unlike most of us whose forebears were not natives of this country, but who came to this country by choice, the Dene have had no real choice as to whether or not they should become Canadians and join this nation state. Their membership in the juridical nation state is not founded on consent but on a combination of coercion and trickery. In not the dimmest of senses were they party to any Canadian social contract. In noting this, I am reminded of what Edmund Burke said about British rule in India.

There is a sacred veil to be drawn over the beginnings of all Governments.
Ours in India had an origin like those which time has sactified by obscurity.
Time, in the origin of most Governments has thrown this mysterious veil
over them; prudence and discretion make it necessary to throw something
of the same drapery over more recent Foundations.

It may be prudent for us to ignore the origins of Canadian rule over native people, including the Dene. But the exercise of such prudence does not mean that we should expect they, the native people, to ignore those origins. Nor does it mean that we, non-native Canadians, should deliberately distort their submission to Canadian sovereignty into its opposite simply because it is given grudgingly and is now accompanied with requests, couched in the language they have learned from us, for a maximum degree of self-government within this sovereign nation. To so distort and twist their words and intentions is a most cynical way to respond to a plea to be treated with more justice by the acknowledged Canadian sovereign.

The main end which the Dene seek is their survival as a distinct ethnic entity, a distinct people, and in that sense a distinct nation or national group within the Canadian state. The Dene propose two basic instruments for securing this end: first, legislative recognition, rather than extinguishment, of collective title to their historic homeland; and secondly, a devolution of governmental authority to their communal organizations. The first, legislative recognition of ownership, is, I take it, essential to their cultural survival. Their land is their life; for it to be parcelled out for sale and exploitation on the commercial market is to alienate them from the essential physical base of their spiritual existence. The need for a devolution of decision-making responsibility to Dene institutions of regional and local government is based primarily on the assumption that the proprietorial rights of a land owner, whether collective (as in the Dene's case) or individual, will be worth very little if the land owner is denied a crucial role in making the most significant decisions about how the land is used and developed. The devolution of a wide range of governmental responsibilities to Dene institutions is also desired as a means of preserving and fostering those aspects of Dene culture which are best expressed through the communal institutions of the Dene.

The precise powers to be delegated to Dene institutions and the relationship of these institutions to the existing territorial and local governments, to any future province which may be established in the region, and to the Parliament of Canada, have not been spelled out in detail. Clearly, these are matters which have to be worked out in negotiations between the Dene people and the federal government. Without pre-judging the results of such negotiations, we can still ask whether a land settlement along the general lines proposed by the Dene is impossible within the Canadian constitutional system. Those general lines are:

1 the main aim of any land settlement is the survival of the Dene people as a distinct cultural and social entity (i.e., a nation) within Canada;
2 the two basic means for securing that end are:
a legislative recognition of the Dene's collective ownership of their historic homeland;
b devolution of governmental responsibility to Dene communal institutions which will have a decisive voice in determining what happens on the homeland.

There is a whole spectrum of possible arrangements which might be proposed within these general parameters. At one extreme are those which would grant the Dene more power and responsibility than the federal government politically, or possibly constitutionally, could consider granting, and at the other extreme are such limited concessions to the Dene's claims that for the Dene to accept them would be to agree to their own extinction as a people. The purpose of negotiating a land settlement of the type proposed by the Dene would be precisely to explore what alternatives exist between these extremes. The question is whether any settlement consistent with the basic requirements of the Dene Declaration is consistent with the Canadian constitution.

Our 'written' constitution, the BNA Act (and its amendments) does not prescribe the arrangements which should be made for Canada's aboriginal people. The BNA Act makes only one direct reference to native people and that is subsection 24 of section 91 which gives the Parliament of Canada exclusive legislative authority in all matters relating to 'Indians and lands reserved for the Indians.' The constitution does not stipulate how Parliament should exercise this grant of legislative power over Indians and their lands. There is a clear implication that this constitutional grant of power to Parliament entails an obligation to protect the interests of Canada's native people. Laskin's text, *Canadian Constitutional Law*, refers to s.91 (24) as a 'specification that Indians as a class should be under federal protection (Abel). Indeed, it would have been illogical for the framers of the constitution to designate Indians as a special class of people under exclusive federal jurisdiction unless they intended that their interests should be protected from the legislative policies of the different provinces.

There is another section of the BNA Act which may extend special constitutional protection to the rights and interests of natives living in that part of Canada which was formerly Rupert's Land and the Northwestern Territory. This is section 146, which provides that the terms of any order in council admitting these territories to the Dominion of Canada become part of the Canadian constitution as if these terms were enacted (as was the BNA Act) by the Parliament of the United Kingdom. The Addresses of the Canadian Parliament petitioning the Queen to transfer Rupert's Land and the Northwestern Territory to Canada and the schedules to the order in council effecting the transfer, recognize the Indians' ownership of their land in these territories and the obligation of the Canadian government to compensate the Indians for any of such lands taken for purposes of settlement 'in conformity with the equitable principles which have uniformly governed the British Crown in its dealings with the Aborigines' (Schedule to the Order-in-Council of 1870). Mr Justice Morrow of the Supreme Court of the Northwest Territories has held that '... the assurances made by the Canadian Government to pay compensation and the recognition of Indian claims by virtue of s.146 of the BNA Act became part of the Canadian Constitution and could not be removed or altered except by Imperial Statute.' For these reasons, he concludes 'that the Indians living within that part of Canada covered by the proposed caveat may have a constitutional guarantee that no other Canadian Indians have' (*Re Paulette*). While Justice Morrow's decision in this case has been successfully appealed to the Court of Appeal of the NWT, this part of his judgment was not reviewed by the Court of Appeal. The Court of Appeal's judgment deals solely with the question of whether a caveat can be filed against Crown lands and does not touch upon the constitutional point in Justice Morrow's decision.

The BNA Act, then, explicitly bestows legislative jurisdiction over Indians and their lands on the federal Parliament and implicitly recognizes an obligation on the part of the federal government to protect the interests and rights of Indian people. Beyond this it is silent on the precise ways and means whereby the federal government is to discharge its responsibilities with regard to native people. Certainly there can be no suggestion that recognition of the basic claims of the Dene Declaration would not be consistent with those sections of our constitution which bear directly on the treatment of native people.

But the other possibility must now be canvassed: namely, that the terms of the constitution which are concerned not directly with indigenous people but with the structure of government generally in Canada would be violated by a land settlement designed to meet the principles of the Dene Declaration. There are two possibilities which must be considered here: first, the recognition of Dene claims within a federal territory, and secondly, the recognition of such a claim in the territory organized as a province.

As far as the structure of territorial government is concerned, the federal Parliament is not tied by the constitution to any precise set of governmental arrangements. Indeed, under its constitutional authority to legislate for the peace, order, and good government of Canada, Parliament has provided a wide range of governmental arrangements over the years, beginning with the Act of 1869 (SC, 32-33 Vic., c.3) establishing a temporary system of administrative control for Rupert's Land and the Northwestern Territory, right up to the establishment of the contemporary Territorial Council under the Northwest Territories Act in 1970 (RSC 1970, c.N-22). It is certainly within the Canadian Parliament's 'peace, order, and good government' power, as well as its explicit power over Indians and lands reserved for Indians, to restructure the territorial government so as to delegate a measure of self-government to Dene institutions which might be established in the territory on Dene lands. Federal legislation providing for such a delegation would be just that, federal legislation, and as such not a constitutional guarantee. However, some 'manner and form' requirements could be attached to such legislation (e.g., the requirement that a two-thirds majority be required to amend the legislation) which might provide a measure of 'entrenchment' (Marshall, Tarnopolsky).

Federal legislation restricting participation in Dene institutions to those of a certain racial heritage might be objected to on the quasi-constitutional grounds that it violates the Canadian Bill of Rights. Such an objection would not be well founded. In the *Drybones* case, the only occasion on which the discrimination and 'equality before the law' phrases of the Bill of Rights were deemed by the Supreme Court to override a section of the Indian Act, the Court's ruling specified 'that an individual is denied equality before the law if it is made an offence punishable at law, for him to do something which his fellow Canadians are free to do without having committed any offence or having been made subject to any penalty.' Legislation recognizing the Dene's ownership of their land and providing institutions of local self-government could not be construed as inflicting criminal punishment on Dene people for reasons of race. Furthermore, as the Supreme Court's decision in *Lavell* indicates, and as has been cogently argued by P.W. Hogg, because Indians are recognized as a special constitutional classification in the BNA Act, such a classification should not be deemed in violation of the 'equality before the law' guarantee in the Bill of Rights.

There would appear then to be no constitutional barrier to Parliament's accommodating the Dene claim within a territorial context. But what about a provincial context? Here the question is whether the Dene's rights to ownership of their land and self-governing institutions could be constitutionally accommodated within a possible future province established in the territory. There can be no question that under our constitution very specific limitations and conditions can be attached to the powers of newly created provinces. Many precedents may be cited but perhaps the most apt are the retention of the natural resources by the Dominion when the prairie provinces joined the federation, and the agreements entered into in 1929 and 1930, and confirmed by the BNA Act of 1930, turning over the natural resources to the provinces, subject to certain lands being set aside for Indian reserves and the protection of Indian hunting and fishing rights. These constitutional agreements clearly gave constitutional protection to Indians in these provinces against provincial legislation (although not, it would appear, against federal legislation). Constitutionally, there is no bar to the Dene's ownership of their land, and their right to participate in Dene institutions of local government can be guaranteed by the terms under which a new province is established.

On the basis of the letter of our constitutional law, there is no legal obstacle to recognition of the Dene claim. Nor, of course, is there any explicit provision for such recognition. The question of whether or not it should be recognized is, fundamentally, one of will and intention, not one of law. Again, to quote Edmund Burke when he was debating with his countrymen two hundred years ago whether or not under the British constitution the American colonists could enjoy the benefits of representative government:

The question with me is not whether you have a right to render your people miserable, but whether it is not in your interest to make them happy. It is not what a lawyer tells me I may do but what humanity, reasons and justice tell me I ought to do.

In deciding a question of this kind, we should look behind the letter of our constitutional text and consider the spirit of our constitution - the philosophy of government and the principles of justice on which it is based. If we do this, I think we can see how arrangements designed to ensure the collective survival of the Dene people entail the extension of the original spirit of Confederation for the first time to Canada's native people.

Confederation was necessary in 1867 because an alternative solution to the governance of French and English 'Canadians' had failed. The alternative solution to Confederation was a programme of assimilation - of assimilation of all Canadians into the British culture. Lord Durham's Report in 1839 called for this solution and the Act of Union in 1840 established a framework of government designed to promote this solution. But it did not work. The majority of French-Canadians would not be assimilated. In 1867, it was Cartier's ideal of pluralistic cultural survival within a single juridical nation, not Durham's ideal of a British nation in North America, which inspired the establishment of a federal system of government guaranteeing the rights of certain minorities within the major units of the new federation. (Here I refer in particular to s.93 of the BNA Act.) Creating the institutions of this new mode of government and making them work has been a major challenge to Canadian statescraft. With its diffusion of governmental authority and its lack of ethnic homogeneity the Confederation system has not been an easy one in which to govern, but it may well be the most liberal mode of self-government for a large continental nation state that the world has known.

What is called for now by the Dene people is the application to them of the spirit of Confederation and the ingenuity of Canadian statescraft in implementing that liberal spirit. It is possible to respond to this call by saying 'We do not know precisely what you want. In any case, we know that it would entail something very different from our established policies and procedures for achieving your assimilation. Therefore we refuse to even talk to you about your objectives or take your claim seriously.' While it may be possible to respond this way without violating the letter of the Canadian constitution, I question whether it is possible to make this response without violating the ideals on which that constitution is based.

I come, finally, to the question of whether a settlement with the Dene should be made before or after the construction of the Mackenzie Valley pipeline. From a purely legal point of view, setting aside any influence which social and economic circumstances may have on constitutional possibilities, a settlement can be made at any time, providing there are two parties who wish to negotiate a settlement.

But, of course, the impact of social circumstances in the real world on the availability of legal alternatives cannot be set aside. One very clear *outside* limit on the time in which a settlement must be negotiated is that both parties to the settlement must survive the period preceding the settlement. From what we know about the advance of our industrial, metropolitan culture on North America's aboriginals, the Dene people, *as a people* with a capacity for expressing and developing their own interests, would not long survive the major social and economic upheavals introduced by the pipeline if their right to survive and institutions to achieve that right were not established. Thus, at a certain point, a few years I would judge, after the pipeline construction had commenced, no settlement with the Dene people would be possible, because there would not be *a people* with which to settle.

But this indicates only an outside limit on the timing of a settlement. Considerably prior to this is the time at which, and the circumstances under which, the Dene have a genuine opportunity to enter into negotiations for the kind of settlement they seek. At the centre of the Dene claim for a land settlement is the objective of influencing, if not deciding, what happens on their traditional homeland. A project such as the proposed pipeline, one of the largest industrial projects ever undertaken in Canadian history, is about as significant a development as one can imagine happening on anyone's land. To tell the Dene that they could negotiate land claims after the pipeline has commenced is at least to tell them that they are to have no opportunity to negotiate for the type of settlement they are seeking. After the pipeline, the Dene's negotiating options are likely to be precisely those of the native people in northern Quebec following the initiation of the James Bay hydro-electric project. A decision by the federal government to commence the pipeline before negotiating a land settlement with the Dene probably represents a final decision to preclude any possibility of considering a land settlement along the lines desired by the Dene people.

There is another reason why the commencement of the pipeline before *any* settlement with the Dene people would not only be gravely prejudicial to the Dene's rights but also would violate a fundamental precept of Canadian government – the rule of law. Canadian law, at least since the *Calder* case, has recognized the existence of aboriginal rights to lands held and occupied since time immemorial until such rights are extinguished by the sovereign Parliament. In the case of the Dene's aboriginal right to their homeland, there is great doubt as to whether that right has been extinguished. Although a literal reading of Treaties 8 and 11 indicates that the Indians did 'cede, release, surrender and yield up' to the government of Canada 'all their rights, titles and privileges whatsoever' to their lands, a great deal of evidence has been amassed to support the contention that these treaties were, in effect, fraudulent and that they cannot be taken seriously as an expression of agreement between two parties. Justice Morrow's finding in the caveat case that the facts cast sufficient doubt on whether aboriginal title was extinguished by treaty to justify a claim for title by the Indian as caveators was based on such evidence, and this aspect of his judgment has not been overruled by the Court of Appeal. Thus, the ownership of the lands over which the pipeline is to be built is not settled in Canadian law. If the federal government permitted the pipeline to proceed in these circumstances before working out a land settlement with the Dene people, it would be determining what is to happen on land whose ownership is in dispute. Constitutionally, Parliament in the end can, if it wishes, authorize the extinguishment of aboriginal rights, just as it can pass modern legislation recognizing those rights. But for the federal government to proceed as if it had no obligation to deal clearly and explicitly with claims based upon aboriginal rights would be to ignore the established procedures of the Canadian legal system as if it were literally 'above the law.' Federal action of this kind would ignore the basis for the Dene claims established in our system of law and in the process violate the 'rule of law,' a fundamental postulate of our constitutional structure.

To sum up, the type of land settlement which the Dene people wish to negotiate with the federal government, far from violating Canada's constitution, calls for the extension to them of the fundamental principle underlying Confederation. The working out of the institutional solutions required to accomplish the purpose would be a major challenge to Canadian statescraft. In a sense this task entails the completion of Confederation by applying, for the first time, the liberal philosophy of ethnic partnership, to our native people. There are no *a priori* constitutional reasons for not attempting this task. On the contrary, if the government understands the ideals upon which our constitutional system is based and wished all of our citizens to participate in those ideals, it is imperative that it not refuse to negotiate a land settlement of the kind envisaged in the Dene Declaration.

Further, I have argued that the opportunity to work out this kind of settlement will be thoroughly undermined if the pipeline is allowed to proceed before a settlement with the people through whose historic homeland this pipeline will pass. Constitutional options are always shaped by historical events and material circumstances. This will be denied by those who have much to gain by precipitating events which will dramatically alter the material circumstances in the Mackenzie Valley hoping to eliminate certain constitutional and legal alternatives in the process. But such a denial is not creditable.

A settlement whose purpose is to ensure the Dene people the right to determine what goes on on their land would scarcely be a meaningful possibility after a project of the mammoth proportions of a pipeline has, independently of the Dene, been initiated on their land. There is the additional objection that for the federal government to by-pass normal legal processes and permit a pipeline to proceed through land the ownership of which is a matter of serious legal dispute, is to set an example of lawlessness by its own behaviour which would serve as an unfortunate model for those whom it must persuade to use lawful means to secure their ends.

REFERENCES

Abel, A.S., *Laskin's Canadian Constitutional Law*, 4th ed. (Toronto, 1973)
Driedger, Elmer A., *A Consolidation of the British North America Acts, 1867 to 1965* (Ottawa 1967)
Forsey, Eugene, 'Canada: Two Nations or One?' *Canadian Journal of Economics and Political Science* (1962)
Hayes, C.J.H., *Essays on Nationalism* (New York, 1926)
Heiman, George, 'The Nineteenth Century Legacy: Nationalism or Patriotism?' in Peter H. Russell, ed., *Nationalism in Canada* (Toronto, 1966)
Hogg, P.W., 'The Canadian Bill of Rights – Equality before the Law: A.G. Can. *v.* Lavell,' 52 *Canadian Bar Review* 263 (1974)
Marshall, Geoffrey, *Constitutional Theory* (Oxford, 1971)
Tarnopolsky, Walter S., *The Canadian Bill of Rights* (Toronto, 1975)
Waite, P.B., ed., *Confederation Debates in the Province of Canada 1865* (Toronto, 1963)

CASES CITED

Re Paulette (1973) 6 WWR 97; rev'd NWT CA, 12 Nov. 1975
The Queen v. *Drybones* (1970) SCR 282
A.-G. Canada v. *Lavell* (1974) SCR 1349
Calder v. *A.-G. British Columbia* (1973) SCR 313

Conclusions

We the Dene

Georges Erasmus

The main issue facing the Dene is not the proposed Mackenzie Valley pipeline or some such other colonial development. The issue facing us today is the same issue that has confronted us since the first non-Dene arrived in our land. The issue is recognition of our national rights, recognition of our right to be a self-governing people.

Throughout the world, various peoples are asserting their right to be self-determining nations. Many Third World peoples are recognizing that their own 'underdevelopment,' their own political, economic, and social dependencies, are directly related to the 'overdevelopment' of the industrialized world. The nationalism of the Third World is a sign of hope for man's ability to build a more just and humanizing world order. People who were once confused and degraded by an experience of colonialism have declared their right to be regarded as self-determining peoples. They have declared their right to be more than just the objects of exploitation.

Within the industrialized nation-states, there exist nations of aboriginal peoples who do not share the wealth and power of the dominant society. These people have a history of exploitation by the developed countries similar to the Third World experience. The difference is that these people exist within the geographical boundaries of the 'developed world.' George Manuel, former president of the National Indian Brotherhood and President of the World Council of Indigenous Peoples, has called such domestic colonies the 'Fourth World.' We the Dene are acutely aware of our colonial relationship with North American society, and are struggling to achieve recognition of our right to be a self-determining people.

Long before Europeans decided to look for resources and riches outside of their own boundaries, the Dene nation existed. We had our own way of life, we had our own laws by which we governed ourselves, by which we lived together – laws for educating young people, laws for respecting old people, laws respecting our land. We had our own ways of worship and our own economic system. We had a complete way of life. We ourselves decided what was best for us and for our land.

The history of a people is the record of the choices they make over time. Before the coming of the Europeans, we the Dene made choices based on our experience. We made our own history. Our actions were based on our understanding of the world.

With the coming of the Europeans, our experience as a people changed. We experienced relationships in which we were made to feel inferior. We were treated as incompetent to make decisions for ourselves. Europeans would treat us in such a way as to make us feel that they knew, better than we ourselves, what was good for us. Those who presented themselves as 'superior' began to define what was good for us. They began to define our world for us. They began to define us as well. Even physically, our communities and our landmarks were named in terms foreign to our understanding. We were no longer the actors – we were being acted upon. We were no longer naming the world – we were being named. We were named 'Indian,' we were being called 'non-status and status Indians' or 'Metis.'

All of these names were imposed on us. We have always called ourselves 'Dene.' Simply translated, we defined ourselves as 'people,' as different from the animals. With the coming of the Europeans, we developed the term 'Dene' to mean not only ourselves as a people separate from the animals, but ourselves as separate from the Europeans.

Traditionally, we acted; today, we are acted upon. Our history since contact is the record of our struggle to act on our own terms. It is the record of our struggle to decide for ourselves as a people in the face of all the forces which have attempted to decide for us, define us, and act for us.

When our ancestors entered the agreements now known as Treaties 8 and 11, it was understood that our right to be a self-determining people had been recognized. The records show that repeatedly, throughout the valley, our leaders told the treaty commissioner, that if signing the treaties meant that this was not our land, or that we would have to follow someone else's laws, then they would never be signed. In some cases, the signatures were forged. In others, the repeated assurances of the bishop satisfied our leaders that recognition of our right to self-determination on our land had been satisfactorily negotiated. The agreements reached by our leaders and the negotiators for the Crown were not land cession agreements. Rather, they were understood as agreements by which our nation would live in peace and friendship with the non-Dene.

Clearly, these agreements have been broken. Instead of recognition of our national right to self-determination, we have been subjected to over fifty years of colonization, of forced assimilation. This experience has had a profound effect on us as a people. Whereas traditionally our laws were agree-

ments we made amongst ourselves, today we see 'laws' as something someone
else imposes on us. Traditionally, we educated our own; today 'education' is
what someone else does to our children, often by forcibly removing them
from their own families.

Today, after over half a century of colonial experience, we have begun to
reassess, as a people, the kind of future we want for ourselves. We recognize
that we do have a choice. We can remain colonized, or we can struggle for the
recognition of our national rights. Assimilation is not without some attrac-
tion, especially to some of the young and educated. It offers individual material gain and some power for those few who might 'make it' in the non-Dene
world. But clearly, only a very few would ever actually 'make it': the majority
of our people would become lost and depressed, similar to the fate of other
North American Indian nations. Assimilation would mean an end forever to
the collective understanding of ourselves as a unique people and our collective
self-determination. Instead, as a people we have been developing an awareness
of our colonized condition, and a determination to struggle to regain our
rights.

In 1974, at the joint general assembly of the Indian Brotherhood and Metis
Association in Fort Good Hope, we formally rejected the concept of a 'land
settlement' which would extinguish our rights. We agreed to work together
as one people - as Dene, rather than accepting the divisions of Metis, Non-
Status, and Treaty which have been imposed on us.

In July, 1975, at the joint general assembly in Fort Simpson, we passed
the Dene Declaration. We publicly declared what we have always known to be
true - that we are a nation of people with the right to self-determination.
More important, the Dene Declaration is the expression of our collective decision after years of colonialism to resist further assimilation and instead to
struggle to regain our freedom as a people.

Our task now is working out the arrangement by which we as a Dene
nation can enter the Confederation of Canada with the guarantee that there
will be an end to attempts to colonize and assimilate us. What agreement can
we reach with the federal government whereby we, as a self-determining people, become a recognized entity within Canada? What form of government do
we require for ourselves?

One possibility is the option of getting limited 'special rights' within a
broader provincial system. Such an option might mean a guaranteed representation in a future provincial legislature, as well as guaranteed 'Dene seats'
at the municipal level. What are the risks of such an option? Suppose we were
guaranteed several seats provincially; there are the dangers of eventually being
outnumbered in our own land, and consequently, effectively losing the con-

trol we need for ourselves. There is another danger as well. The experience of George Barnaby, now vice-president of the Indian Brotherhood of the NWT but previously a Territorial Councillor, has shown us that even if we are represented on Territorial Council the form and procedure is foreign to our own values and decision-making process. Rather than being able to represent the Dene interest in decisions, the structure dictates the evolution of elitist decision-making – 'for' the people, rather than 'by' the people. Territorial Council, for instance, passed a motion in support of the proposed pipeline, after every single community affected had strongly declared its opposition to the project. Such a solution seems, therefore, to be really just neo-colonial. A few Dene would become part of the system which has exploited our people, and instead of changing that system, they themselves would become exploiters! Neocolonial solutions are not acceptable to us.

What are the risks instead, of opting for our own 'Dene government' within Confederation? Such an option would mean setting up our own system with political jurisdiction over a defined land base. International experience tells us that the self-determination of a people is essential for that people to survive as an integral entity – as a nation. A Dene government, with the right to amend and develop that government as we as a people develop, would give us assurance of our ability to be a self-determining and independent people within Canada.

At the moment, the federal government does not even recognize our right to exist collectively. Professor Dosman, in his book *The National Interest*, documents the fact that the federal government consciously chose to promote pipeline development as quickly as possible in the hopes that pipeline construction would begin before we could effectively organize to assert our rights. In other words, the government is aware of our rights, but has chosen to undermine them in favour of colonial development.

Nevertheless, we have been struggling for a long time now, and we must make sure that neither blatantly, by a James Bay type of agreement, nor subtly over time, can our right to national self-determination be subverted. Continuing colonialism or neo-colonialism, regardless of its form, is not acceptable to us. We want to be an independent and self-determining people within Canada, nothing less.

Our ancestors thought that they had reached just such an agreement with the non-Dene at the time of the first treaties. When we began to realize that the understanding we reached with the Government of Canada was being subverted, that our nation was under siege, we began a collective struggle to reassert our rights. At that time, we organized the Indian Brotherhood and soon commenced an action in the courts, resulting in the decision of Justice Morrow to the effect that we do in fact have a legal interest in the land we call ours. Just recently we have begun a process of decolonization, focusing our attention on our recent colonial experience to understand the extent to which our independence has been undermined. From that understanding we can plan actions to free ourselves again.

It was at this point in time that Judge Berger entered our nation's history. Some non-Dene have suggested that Judge Berger is our 'last hope.' It is quite true that the Berger Inquiry has happened at an important time in Dene history and that there is great respect for the manner in which Judge Berger has carried out his Inquiry. Nevertheless, it is a misunderstanding to see Judge Berger, or any other non-Dene, as our 'last hope.' We have made the Berger Inquiry a success by choosing to use it as a forum to declare our intention to struggle for our national rights, and Mr Berger in return has contributed to the growth of our collective self-awareness. Whatever the outcome of his report, we will continue this work long after he is gone. In the end, we are our last hope. The truth of the matter is that those who see the Berger Inquiry as our last hope are accepting the colonialism which has been imposed on us. They are suggesting that only the colonizers can act: the colonized can only 'hope' that someone else will act for them.

It can never be true of any oppressed people that their interests will be represented by others than themselves. It is only we, the Dene, who can guarantee our future. It is only by our actions that we can get the kind of agreement we must have with the federal government. The Dene nation, we as Dene people, will survive as long as we are collectively struggling and acting to define the world in our own terms. Only we can de-colonize ourselves.

That does not mean that our struggle is not of interest or significance to non-Dene. The basic human rights for which we are struggling, the right to be self-determining, are universal rights. We believe that our struggle is in the interest of all Canadians. We welcome the support of all Canadians in telling the federal government that there must be official recognition of our right to be a self-determining people within the Confederation of Canada.

A Proposal to the Government and People of Canada

Agreement in Principle between the Dene Nation and Her Majesty the Queen, in right of Canada

A proposal presented to the government and people of Canada on 25 October 1976

Preamble

... In 1899 and 1921, our nation made two treaties with the non-Dene. For our forefathers, the treaties were an agreement with the non-Dene whereby we would live in peace and mutual respect, whereby our right to continued self-determination would be guaranteed. In Dene society, men related to men by agreement. We understood that a man was measured by how he kept his word. The agreement that our forefathers made verbally with the Government of Canada was that our right to self-determination shall never be violated '... as long as the world does not change, as long as the sun continues, as long as the river continues to flow, as long as this land shall last.' It was not until the late 1960s that we became aware of the meaning of the written versions of Treaties 8 and 11.

By fraud, the written versions contained conditions never agreed to by our forefathers: 'the said Indians do hereby cede, release, surrender and yield up to the Government of the Dominion of Canada, for His Majesty the King and His Successors for ever, all their rights, titles, and privileges whatsoever to the lands included within the following limits' ...

It is over half a century since the time of the first treaties between our nation and non-Dene. Now, both the Government of Canada and the Dene Nation are seeking to make a new agreement, a treaty which will be respected and lasting for both parties.

Our experience has taught us that it is foolhardy to expect anyone other than ourselves to protect our interests. We must have more than an assurance that our interests will be taken care of by others, or by the institutions of others. Relationships whereby one party undertakes to protect the interests of others are by definition colonial. Therefore, we insist on the right to define, protect and present our own interest.

This means that we must have our own exclusive political jurisdiction within Canada. We must have our own political institutions through which we both govern ourselves internally as we choose, and continue to present our collective interests externally to the rest of Canada. Only with our own exclusive political jurisdiction can we meet these requirements. Unless these requirements are met, it is meaningless to talk to the Dene as a people, or Dene Culture, being a continuing reality. Any other arrangement would be genocide.

Our right to self-government within the Confederation of Canada must be the basis of our new agreement with the Federal Government. Basic to that right is the recognition to exclusive Dene political jurisdiction over areas of primary important to our life as a people ...

We have recently come to grips with the implications of living in a world in which men make decisions not by agreement but by manipulation of power. The lesson of the Treaties and the lesson of our experience since that time is that our rights will not be adequately protected by assurances of non-Dene institutions, be they corporations or the Federal Government. Our rights will only be protected by the assertion of those rights by ourselves. This lesson, above all, has made it clear that we must govern ourselves through our own exclusive institutions and must have the ability not simply to negotiate an agreement, once and for all, with the Federal Government, but an ability to negotiate the terms of all activities affecting our interests long into the future. This is why recognition, not extinguishment, of rights in the form of an exclusive Dene jurisdiction or government is the first principle of our position.

We cannot understand how anyone could seriously suggest that we would consider negotiating the extinguishment of our rights. What we insist upon is a departure from the tradition in Canada that rights must be extinguished. We want our property rights to our land recognized and preserved, not extinguished. Such recognition of Aboriginal land has happened elsewhere in the world and we cannot see why it cannot happen here.

However, our rights are more than property rights. We have important human rights recognized in International Laws, such as the right to self-determination as a people.

Our struggle, like oppressed and colonized people everywhere, is the assertion of the right to recognition and self-determination as people. Our demands are the recognition and protection of those important human rights which have been secured by other peoples. We are a nation of the fourth world, the world of aboriginal peoples within the framework of independent, nation states.

This is not separatism. It means self-reliance and self-determination as people within Canada. It means a reclarification of our rights and a negotiation of our place in confederation in the context of a Dene Government. We know that this is in the spirit of the Canadian constitution and that there is no reason why the tradition of extinguishment has to be followed. We can never agree to the extinguishment of ourselves as a people ...

Constitutional recognition, that is, recognition of the right of the Dene to govern themselves through institutions of their choosing, would be insufficient to ensure Dene independence and the development of the Dene as a people. Colonialism is not simply a matter of political control but is also a matter of economic and social relationships ...

Clearly, we must develop our own economy, rather than depending on externally initiated development. Such an economy would not only encourage continued renewable resource activities, such as hunting, fishing and trapping but would include community-scale activities designed to meet our needs in a more self-reliant fashion. True Dene development will entail political control, an adequate resource base, and continuity with our past. It will be based on our own experience and values. In accordance with our emphasis on sharing, Dene development will not permit a few to gain at the expense of the whole community ...

While the Dene have certain Aboriginal Rights not shared by non-Dene, the basic human struggle is shared by all who are working for a world not based on man's exploitation of man. It is therefore contradictory for us not to deal with how the Dene struggle affects the rights of others.

Almost all non-Dene who have come to our land have come directly or indirectly as the agents of institutions seeking some form of control over us. The Government of Canada must bear full responsibility for having encouraged and misled such people into believing that they had the right to exploit our land and to colonize us as a people. Our new agreement with the Federal Government will mean that such colonizing forces shall stop.

Nevertheless, the reality is that there are now many non-Dene in our land, and what we seek is a peaceful relationship with these people, based on recognition of our right and their right to self-determination.

Because most non-Dene live in a few concentrated urban centres, to assist the Federal Government in its responsibilities towards these people, we are willing to allow such centres to exist outside the jurisdiction of Dene institutions. In return, the Federal Government must agree to establish new communities for the Dene of such centres, as the Dene involved may choose ...

The written version of the first treaties represents a non-negotiated agreement. Essentially, the written version of the treaties is a unilateral declaration of the Federal Government's position which it has since attempted to impose without agreement on the Dene.

In seeking a new agreement, it is assumed that both parties have an interest in reaching a truly negotiated understanding rather than a unilateral imposition of terms by one party on the other ...

For the Federal Government to suggest that it is prepared to 'negotiate' only if the purpose of negotiations is the extinguishment of Dene rights is a cynical contradiction. Obviously, it is not of benefit to the Dene to negotiate the extinction of their interest. In fact, it is doubtful that the term 'negotiations' could ever be applied to a situation where one party seeks to extinguish the rights of the other.

In the written version of the original treaties, the Federal Government's position was extinguishment of rights. The James Bay settlement and the Federal proposal to the Yukon Council of Indians suggest that that position may not have changed very much over the past half-century. Therefore, in order that the Government of Canada and the Dene Nation can seriously begin to negotiate a new agreement, the Dene are now proposing that agreement first be reached on the principles and purpose of negotiations. Such an Agreement in Principle will establish explicitly the common assumptions on which further negotiations will be based ...

The Agreement in Principle specifies the principles which the Dene consider to be an essential basis for further negotiations. The Signing of the Agreement in Principle will represent a progressive step in that both the Dene and the Federal Government will have reached agreement on the basis for further negotiations. It is in the interest of the Dene, the Federal Government, and the General Public that negotiations proceed as quickly as possible towards a final agreement ...

Agreement in principle between the Dene Nation and Her Majesty the Queen, in right of Canada

WHEREAS prior to the coming of the Europeans the Dene, the aboriginal people of the Mackenzie Valley, have lived on their traditional lands since time immemorial;

AND WHEREAS the Dene have certain property rights to their traditional lands;

AND WHEREAS Europeans and other non-Dene have settled upon and undertaken developments upon the traditional lands of the Dene without an agreement or treaty between the Dene and non-Dene Canadians;

AND WHEREAS confusion exists as to the meaning of Treaties 8 and 11;

AND WHEREAS there are in International Law certain political, human and universal rights such as the rights to self-determination, non-discrimination, and enjoyment of culture which are witnessed in the practice of nations and international instruments such as the United Nations' Declaration of Human Rights;

AND WHEREAS the Dene have survived as a people;

AND WHEREAS both the Dene and the Government of Canada have expressed a desire to see clarification of the rights of the Dene and the negotiation of a new agreement or treaty between the Dene and other Canadians at the earliest possible occasion;

IT IS THEREFORE AGREED between the Dene and the Government of Canada that negotiations do commence forthwith to resolve the aforesaid according to the following principles:

1 The Dene have the right to recognition, self-determination, and on-going growth and development as a People and as a Nation.

2 The Dene, as aboriginal people, have a special status under the Constitution of Canada.

3 The Dene, as aboriginal people, have the right to retain ownership of so much of their traditional lands, and under such terms, as to ensure their independence and self-reliance, traditionally, economically and socially, and the maintenance of whatever other rights they have, whether specified in this agreement or not.

4 The definition of the Dene is the right of the Dene. The Dene know who they are.

5 The Dene have the right to practice and preserve their languages, traditions, customs and values.

6 The Dene have the right to develop their own institutions and enjoy their rights as a People in the framework of their own institutions.

7 There will therefore be *within* Confederation, a Dene Government with jurisdiction over a geographical area and over subject matters now within the jurisdiction of either the Government of Canada or the Government of the Northwest Territories.

8 The Government of Canada hereafter in the exercise of matters within its jurisdiction (and following a settlement with the Dene) will:

(a) abandon the 'last frontier' mentality and all attempts to colonize and settle Dene lands; and

(b) do everything in its power to assist in the recognition, survival, and development of the Dene as a People.

9 The Government of Canada will finance the establishment of new Dene communities in cases where existing communities are inhabited by significant numbers of non-Dene and a significant proportion of the Dene community wishes to re-establish themselves elsewhere.

10 The Dene will be compensated by the Government of Canada for past use of Dene land by non-Dene.

11 Within six months of the signing of this agreement negotiations will commence for a final agreement or treaty, and within six months of the signing of

the final agreement, legislation incorporating the terms of the final agreement will be submitted to Parliament.

12 It is recognized and accepted that negotiations must allow for the ongoing involvement of all Dene.

13 In the interim period between the signing of this agreement and the passing of legislation by Parliament, the parties hereto will not take any actions which violate either the terms or the spirit of this agreement.

AND WHEREAS the Dene recognize that there are non-Dene who have come to live among the Dene and the Dene wish to be fair to them;

AND WHEREAS both the Dene and the Government of Canada wish to recognize and respect the rights of the non-Dene;

AND WHEREAS the Dene recognize that while Territorial Council and municipal councils are governments in the non-Dene tradition, the non-Dene have the right to evolve more democratic forms of institutions based on democracy and equality and the representation of the interests of the masses of non-Dene, not an elite;

IT IS THEREFORE AGREED that the following principles are recognized by the Dene and the Government of Canada:

14 The Dene agree that non-Dene have the right to self-determination and the use and development of their own institutions; and the Dene pledge their support to the non-Dene in the pursuit of their rights.

15 The Government of Canada will establish a regime to compensate all non-Dene who suffer hardship because of, or non-Dene who wish to leave the Northwest Territories because they are unable to adjust to, changes ensuring the viability of the principles herein contained and particularly measures introduced to guarantee the recognition, self-determination, and development of the Dene as a People.

16 The Dene agree that all non-Dene holding lands in estate fee simple as of October 15, 1976 will not be deprived of their property rights, but after that date all lands will be subject to the terms of this agreement.

IN WITNESS WHEREOF, Her Majesty and the Dene through their representatives have hereunto set their hands this   day of   , AD 1976.

Contributors

Michael Asch teaches in the Department of Anthropology, University of Alberta

George Barnaby is vice-president of the Indian Brotherhood of the NWT; he was elected to the Territorial Council as the member from Mackenzie/Great Bear, but resigned while in office

Wilf Bean is a consultant to the Indian Brotherhood of the NWT in Yellowknife; he was previously employed by the government of the NWT

Phillip Blake is a social worker who lives in Fort McPherson

Gerry Cheezie is chief of the Fitz-Smith Band and lives in Fort Smith

Georges Erasmus is president of the Indian Brotherhood of the NWT

John F. Helliwell teaches in the Department of Economics, University of British Columbia

Arvin D. Jelliss is an economic consultant to the Haida, Queen Charlotte Islands, BC and was a consultant to the Indian Brotherhood of the NWT

Steve Kakfwi is director of the pipeline inquiry program for the Indian Brotherhood of the NWT

George Kurzewski lives in Fort Smith and is the president of the local of the Metis Association of the NWT

René Lamothe lives in Fort Simpson and is a former director of the Koe-go-cho Society, a Dene cultural and educational organization

Phoebe Nahanni is the former director of Dene land research for the Indian Brotherhood of the NWT.

Bob Overvold is executive director of the Metis Association of the NWT

Peter Puxley is a consultant to the Indian Brotherhood of the NWT in Yellowknife

Scott Rushforth teaches in the Department of Anthropology, University of New Mexico

Peter H. Russell teaches in the Department of Political Economy, University of Toronto

Charlie Snowshoe is a hunter and trapper from Fort McPherson

C. Gerald Sutton is a lawyer and a consultant to the Indian Brotherhood of the NWT in Yellowknife

Frank T'Seleie lives in Fort Good Hope and is a former chief of the Fort Good Hope Band

Mel Watkins teaches in the Department of Political Economy and University College, University of Toronto and was a consultant to the Indian Brotherhood of the NWT in Yellowknife